TAX TREES

NATIVE AMERICAN

STRATEGIES

TAX TREES

NATIVE AMERICAN

STRATEGIES

by

Robert Robinson

A Bible of Booklets

Vol. 2, Ed. 1

INTRODUCTION

<u>Native American Strategies</u>

"The handbook that teaches Native Americans how to take over the private sector's businesses and pump resources back into their communities!"

Dedication

This work is dedicated to the indigenous people inhabiting the English-speaking world wanting to break free from idiotic foreign imperialists currently occupying their homeland. To all the aboriginal tribes of the New World, South Africa and Oceania: My book is just for you! These Germanic civilizations are destroying our countries with runaway government spending, currency inflation and fire suppression. It's time to take the power back!

Foreword

As a Native American, I have known Robert since he was a young boy. I first met him while working at his stepfather's tax business. From my own personal experience, he truly is an honest, trustworthy, born-again Sabbatarian Christian. What he lacks in education he makes up for in firsthand experience.

This dilemma is a national security issue at the highest. You need to follow these books' directions ASAP! If you don't, Western civilization will fall! TAX TREES is the only plan that can guarantee Native Americans their freedom.

-Nancy Davis

Preface

Native American Strategies is the second volume of the TAX TREES trilogy. My handbook is designed to improve the businesses and personal lives of every Native American. Bible of booklets is a play on words. The Holy Bible uses books as its chapters. Its format inspired my style of writing throughout the entire series. This series originally started as a forestry research project and has become much, much more now! You can read it in any order you want!

Dissolved booklets include Proper Lifestyles, Walks for Individuals, Future Formats, The Sound of Music and Saving the History. They'll guide the Native American private sector through Operation White Wolf. I wanted to save America and be generous, so I hope you'll enjoy 10+ years of my work!

Robert W. Robinson, Jr.
-Author, TAX TREES

TABLE OF CONTENTS

Synopsis

Wolf Initiation

White Wolf

This handbook will guide Native Americans through Operation White Wolf. Operation White Wolf was the first book's plan showing natives how to take back their country within three generations. That volume focused on the government portion of White Wolf while this one focuses on the business end of the plan. My business warfare plan guarantees natives the ability to take complete control of the U.S. private sector.

Trident Plan

Once the natives pass the preparations phase, they're ready for the three steps of execution. The first generation will buy out all the available farmland outside the cities and towns. For the second generation, natives from the towns will infiltrate the service industry while the ones from the cities take over urban manufacturing. The third and final wave liberates the cities' corporate office world, thus ending the war.

Preview

There are four unequally-sized quadrants. Each quadrant is marked by a different repetitive picture seen on their chapters' title pages. The first preps the individuals. Quadrant two covers farming practices while the third handles manufacturing. The final quarter involves the printing industry. Chapters contain overviews and reviews. Overviews are keys unlocking the intel. Without them, you wouldn't understand the information. Reviews demonstrate how to apply the information into our society.

CHAPTER ONE

Spiritual Guidance

Overview

Protection

Description:

This chapter discusses spiritual preparations before going into battle with the Anglo-Saxons. If you don't read this first, you'll be a fool no matter how hard you try not to be. It's impossible to become wise without God. People who don't become born-again and follow his ways are given over to a depraved mind. Then, God will turn you into a homosexual or lesbian to slow down your breeding. Eventually, he'll strike you down and let you burn in Hell forever, the land of nightmares. You'll be powerless against demons and occultists when they levy attacks against you or try to possess you. What's described as the narrow path should've been described as the only path.

Importance:

You'll also be constantly deceived by spirits and the people surrounding you. Your eyes aren't fully open to the cold hard fact that 99% of everyone who has ever lived past, present or future is a scumbag. Without God's hand of blessing, you cannot do anything apart from the vine. He controls everything and you control nothing. All you have is something he gave you or let you hold on to. He empowers you long enough to give you a chance to come back to him. Use this time to repent of your sins. Then, you can change the dying world around by operating through the power of the vine.

Wisdom

Empowerment:

You'll be capable of having dominion over demons and no weapon formed against you shall prosper. With obedience, faith and persistence you'll eventually persevere in any goal you've set for yourself. It's in his Word. Protestant Christianity will make you unstoppable and biblical truth will make you wise enough to resist all the deceit you'll hear around you. It's only when you're capable of becoming spiritually protected, strong and wise that you can move on to the next chapter of my book.

Christianity

Assemblies

The Reverends:

A reverend is a senior pastor who can lead several Protestant assemblies. They're not recent converts, are born again, are monogamists and have families in line with Apostle Paul's teachings. All TV evangelists should be reverends or messianic rabbis.

The Pastors:

A pastor is an ordained minister leading a single service. They have the exact same requirements too. Major independent pastors sometimes evangelize over the radio.

Your Elders:

Elders are ordained ministers with similar requirements. They can lead contemporary and youth services with a soapbox or become an accountant in the office wing. Women can speak freely when working inside of the offices, schools or dating wings.

Your Musicians:

Use male singers in the main halls. Add an organ to the main hall and a live band in the contemporary hall. Women are encouraged to sing during extracurricular events.

Our Ushers:

Ushers are the men who serve as the physical labor arm of the church's organizations.

The Disciples:

The fellowship and recently converted sit in benches called pews. Women can lead women and children in Bible study inside wings. Set up a pulpit for ministers to preach, performing altar calls and deliverance. Speakers of tongues go one at a time.

Our Women:

Women will have long hair and coverings during Saturday service. There are dating classes for widows or virgins in a wing. Wives submit to husbands since women are wife to husband the way men are wife to Christ. Man was created in the image of God first and woman created in the image of man afterward. Our sisters can sing prayers songs. However, *Jude* says there are no new prophecies or doctrines! Ladies without long hair and welcome to don wigs, weaves or extensions. Encourage girls to grow their hair out. Sisters can only hold positions over men outside of the church.

Biblical Truth

Doctrine

Baptism by Fire:

To become born again, call out to God in prayer until you see the Holy Spirit. You might see Jesus with him also. When I woke up one night, I saw a big, glowing ball in the top corner of my room facing my bed. It looked like fog, smoke and was wispy. His voice was like an audible whisper full of power. He had to strengthen me to sit up in his presence. That's the time when you receive the white seal. When the Spirit speaks to you again, the first thing that happens is you'll feel light, colors become more saturated and you feel like you're on downers. A whisper wells up in your chest and you communicate telepathically with him. *Baptism by water is still important.*

Studying the Bible:

First, read the New Testament front-to-back as soon as you can. This is the New Covenant you must follow. Next, read the Old Testament front-to-back to grow in wisdom. When faced with demonic attack, which usually comes shortly thereafter, rebuke the demons in the name of Jesus Christ and pray for the blood of Jesus to cover you. Always try to set aside Saturday as a day of rest and worship. Read the *Holy Bible* and pray every day. Fast a little every year during a crisis. Start your prayers with Father, thank you, repentance, asking for something and ending all of your prayers by saying "in Jesus' name, Selah". Avoid chants; they're not from the heart.

Avoiding Apostasy:

There's only one spiritual father. Spiritual patriarchs were the people who fathered Israel. Levitical priesthood was the only way you could have talked to God during the Old Covenant. The Judges were Israel's rulers before they had kings. God's prophets were picked by God to convince the kings to turn back. The apostles wrote the Gospel and were given the Great Commission. Only God can interpret the Scripture. Alcohol is occasionally recommended by the Holy Bible to aid in digestion or communion. Swearing false oaths to God, not cussing, is the act of taking his name in vain. Idols are statues of false gods. God is the "LORD", spelt in all-caps, while Jesus is "Lord".

Professionalism:

Men shouldn't have hair longer than a bro flow. Women shouldn't have hair shorter than that. Women who are incapable of having long hair due to illnesses aren't penalized. During services, men shall take their hats off. Avoid using foul language.

Pagan Association:

Sometimes, disciples are forced to associate or even dine with unbelievers. If they're coworkers, family, neighbors or potential converts, then it's okay. Avoid bickering with antichrists; only God can change them. Denying Christ in the flesh is antichrist.

Bearing Fruit:

One way to tell if someone is a born-again believer is by their fruit. Good fruit can only come from good trees and bad fruit can only come from bad trees. In this case, fruit is symbolic of the fruit of your labors. Without works, faith is dead. The World keeps getting worse around you and they never do anything about it. They say they will pray for you, but won't get in the trenches with you. Avoid these types of people! Another thing to watch out for when dealing with these people is the "playing dumb" card. The *Bible* says you are without excuse. Most of them are fully-grown adults. They need to own up, take responsibility. Stop spoon-feeding them!

Gospels' Truth:

You're saved by grace since works can't undo your sins. When Apostle Paul discussed the Law, he spoke about the sacrificial laws not including the Ten Commandments. If it's okay to stop following them, then should we carve an idol and worship it as God? Is it acceptable to take the LORD's name in vain on false oaths? Is it okay to dishonor the lowercased version of the sabbath, which is Saturday, because we're in modern times? Apostle Paul stated, "Let anyone who preaches another gospel be damned!"

Alms to the Poor:

If assemblies won't help people, yet spend thousands on billboards or additions, avoid them! Also, stop claiming God hates people. Your assembly is not a political voting platform for political parties! Avoid sales or voting in the assemblies if you can.

Women's Conduct:

Women aren't allowed to hold any authority over a man when they're inside the church. The only grounds for divorce is adultery. If you're not right with your own spouse, it will hinder your prayer life. If you're married to an unbeliever, they're sanctified. If they're abusive, turn into a traitor or do evil, then I don't fault you for leaving. If a woman is divorced and lays with another, they commit adultery. If an ex remarries another, they've committed adultery against their ex. Women need to stay pure and without blemish. Therefore, chastity and beautification are Godly virtues.

True Stewardship:

The first commandment says honor God and those put in authority above you. Jesus paid taxes. The pledge of allegiance to any country is mandatory for its citizens. Remember: To the Jew first, then the Gentile. Anti-Semites are not tolerated. Also, always support Israel. Gentiles aren't bound by the Messianic Jews' kosher diet.

Review

Protection

Your Preparations:

This concludes the first chapter. Your spiritual preparations are nearly complete. The only thing left that you'll need to do is read the entire New Testament before reading the Old Testament. By the time you finish the New Testament, you can operate in the Kingdom of God without qualm. Don't think that you won't require the wisdom of the Old Testament in the modern world; you wouldn't be at your fullest otherwise.

Warnings

Church Heresy:

Beware of the false prophets' heresy and their apostate churches. Do not bicker with them since you can't fix stupid or change their hearts; they made their choices. God reveals his deepest, innermost qualities to everyone past, present or future. If the people you're with aren't born again, cut them out of your life. The only time you should associate with them is if they're business related, relatives, neighbors or people in need. Don't befriend them or associate with them during your personal time. Always check to make sure the spirit around you is of God. The Devil and his forces love to impersonate the Holy Spirit in an attempt to deceive you. Be careful!

Godly Works:

Once you become born again, you can operate in the vine. Plead the blood of Jesus over yourself when facing demonic attack. Prayer and fasting can solve everything. Become born again and study this chapter first. Then, follow the next two chapters of this book. The first three chapters from this book are the *Walks for Individuals* portion of the handbook. The next chapter is the diet and exercise plan. After that, you'll learn how to write professionally and dress for the part. You must complete these steps in order before you can execute the business plans discussed later on.

CHAPTER TWO

Diet and Exercise

Overview

Nutrition

Your Health:

Chapter Two covers your nutritional and exercise plan. Many occupations require immense physical strength that some men don't possess. Also, you need muscular and overall endurance. Otherwise, you'll overtrain, lose physical strength and shrink.

Kosher Diet:

My diet was inspired by the Holy Bible's biblical kosher diet. Unlike the kosher diet, this diet includes pork and doesn't involve the same strict preparation methods. The reason why I am comparing it to that diet is because of its low-fat strategy. I'm not saying you should have a no-fat diet either. You can have sodas, milk shakes and eat sweets. Just make sure you aren't using them as a substitute for the simple sugars found in fruit. *Note: Type I diabetics need to consume less sugar and carbohydrates.*

Balancing Macros:

The diet focuses on trying to create a balance between sugar, carbohydrates and fat. Most people want to have a low-carb diet or a low-fat diet – medium sugar, medium carbs and medium fat. When you're trying to lose weight, make the diet low-fat. If you seek to gain weight, make the diet high-fat. Only adjust fat, not the two sugars. People trying to gain weight need to drink alcohol before hitting the gym. Men trying to lose weight need to reduce their alcohol intake and perform high-intensity cardio.

Fitness

Exercise Plans:

Women will be given a workout plan that's much different than the ones they're used to. They won't become too bulky or lose their curves. Use stretch exercises instead of static stretches when beginning your workouts. Men, start with less volume than is listed. Over time, add more sets in until you've reached what I've listed for you.

Nutrition

Fat

Hierarchy:

Thin Plant Oils: *(Olive Oil, Sunflower Oil)*

Thick Plant Oils: *(Vegetable Oil, Canola Oil)*

Cold Animal Fats: *(Refrigerated Bacon Bits)*

Hot Animal Fats: *(Burgers, Bacon Grease)*

Usage:

Olive Oil: *(Dipping Bread, Vinaigrettes)*

Canola Oil: *(Thick Salad Dressings)*

Corn Oil: *(Frying, Mexican Food)*

Vegetable Oil: *(Tuber Vegetables)*

Lard: *(Mushrooms, Greens, Meat)*

Butter: *(Seafood, Baking/Pastry)*

Margarine: *(Potatoes, Toast)*

Reasons:

Hot Foods:

Each oil has a flash point. You don't want to waste money on expensive oils that boil away too quickly. If you use just enough to wet everything under proper heat, all of the excess oil will boil away. Practice measuring fats first. More experienced cooks can eyeball their hot food measurements. When it comes down to saturated fat and cholesterol, margarine is the lowest and butter is the highest. Animal fats will benefit lower cooking temperatures used on foods like spinach, mushrooms, fish and eggs. Plant oils benefit higher cooking temperatures used on meats and root vegetables.

Baking and Pastry:

Baking and pastry requires precise measurements that cannot be eyeballed. Follow recipes to the tee. Also, if large amounts of animal fats are unhealthy when consumed in hot foods, use them to make compounds instead like bread in baking or pastry. This makes items like butter, lard, shortening or sugarcane less unhealthy to eat.

Meals

Breakfasts are small, light meals. Don't overeat or you could get gas cramps. Just skip breakfast if you don't wake up early enough! Lunch is the largest and lightest meal with more bread and cheese. Dinner is the heaviest meal and is equal to or smaller than lunch. It has the most greens, rice, pasta and tubers. Drink fruit smoothies at home, tea at the gym and sports drinks cut with ice water when working outdoors. Remember, a lack of protein and sugar could result in headaches after lifting weights!

Meats

Steak:

Limit steak dinners to leg or cardio day. Use rosemary, tarragon, thyme, garlic, salt, pepper and steak seasonings. For drinks, pair ales for men and cabernets for women.

Hamburger:

Mix hamburger meat with Italian sauces during pasta night. Flat pastas are for cream sauces with lemon juice, white wine and Italian parsley. Round pastas are for red sauces with Italian seasoning, oregano flakes, marjoram, basil and parsley. Pale ales serve as men's beers. Pair merlots with cream sauces and pinot noirs for red sauces.

Lamb:

This is for your second-lightest day in caloric output. Use rosemary, tarragon, thyme, salt, pepper, garlic and steak seasonings. Pair ales for men and shirazes for women.

Pork:

Pork chops need sage, poultry seasoning, steak seasoning, salt, pepper, garlic, and possible marjoram and savory. Pork dishes pair well with Rieslings and Pilsner beers.

Chicken:

Breasts and dark meat chicken get poultry seasoning, sage, salt, pepper, garlic, thyme and crushed rosemary. Serve a chardonnay or lager with the thighs. Chicken should be the most common dish you eat. The other meal choices are "once-a-week" meals.

Seafood:

Use vegetable and chicken broths cut with water, butter, salt, white pepper, garlic and tarragon. Pair with a sauvignon blanc or pale lager. Use broths on chicken. Limit seafood to one day per week and only use it for your recovery day, aka your rest day.

Vegetarian:

Vegetarian meals with whey protein powder shakes are used during partial fasts.

Vegetables

Onions:

Toss green onions, chives or leeks in at the end. The darker they become, the more overcooked they are. Only use the white core of leeks. Remove the outer layers, chop the green parts and the ends off. Use a dash of oregano powder and onion powder.

Carrots:

Use this exclusively with dill in nearly every single dish. Carrots must go in first since they'll require the most time to cook. Never pair carrots and bell peppers together.

Celery:

Use celery with celery salt and garlic salt in almost every dishes' mixtures. Mirepoix (mixed-veggies) with bell peppers should not use carrots. Just add onions and celery!

Peppers:

Use onion powder and black pepper in International dishes. Roast the skins off with a stove burner, blanch them and sauté. Always pickle peppers when used in salads.

Potatoes:

Use russets for pot roasts, baked potatoes or dishes with radishes. Yukon potatoes are for soups, stews and potato pancakes. Add salt, white pepper, butter and garlic.

Tomatoes:

Use roma, grape or cherry tomatoes sliced bite-sized before cooking. If you don't slice them before cooking, they'll taste awful when they burst in your mouth! For herbs, only add basil. Toss the tomatoes in towards the very end to avoid overcooking them.

Radishes:

Add savory with a dash of butter once your radishes are fully cooked. Toss these in towards the end, but add them to the pan long before the mushrooms or tomatoes.

Parsnips:

Use one parsnip maximum with a dash of marjoram. Cook them during the beginning.

Mushrooms:

Use lard, garlic, onion powder, salt and pepper. Add them right before the tomatoes.

Greens:

*Wilt spinach (not baby) by sticking it in at the end while the flame is turned off.

*Greens can be blanched (shocked and cooled) before adding salt and butter.

Exercise

Training

Pyramiding:

When lifting weights, perform at least two to ten lighter sets before reaching your max. Once you can't do anymore, drop set until you have performed the necessary amount of reps listed. Supersets involve hitting the same muscle group with a different exercise right after finishing another one. Circuit training involves going back and forth from one piece of equipment to the next on the same muscle group.

Overtraining:

Never lift weights for more than 1 ½ hours a day. If a muscle stops feeling sore, give it another day off before hitting it again. Avoid lifting before bedtime or you could suffer from insomnia. If you feel like you have a hot blood pressure headache in the back of your head, take at least one day off. In this situation, you've overtrained your cerebellum. This is the section of your brain that handles all your muscle coordination.

Women

Training Plan:

Women need to construct a workout routine including five to seven exercises per day with one rest day on every third day. Use the same leg workouts, but limit squats to 135 lbs. for petite women and 185 lbs. for taller gals. They should limit leg machine exercises to quarter-stacks for petite women and half-stacks for taller individuals. For lateral raises, petite chicks can use 10 lb. dumbbells and taller people lift 15 lb. ones.

Bodyweight:

All upper-body exercises apart from the lateral raises are bodyweight exercises. This allows women to build maximum strength with the least amount of muscle size possible. Only hit each muscle group once a week for 50-100 reps. You don't want to shrink your breasts too much or develop a gross, rectangular, male-shaped waistline!

Aesthetics:

Only perform cardio one to three times per week with 15 minutes of sprinting. Long incline walks overdevelop your legs and make you look stockier. You need to keep a bodyfat percentage around 18-24% to have soft, thick, creamy skin and nice breasts. Conical bras sculpt ski-sloped boobs. Vacuum poses are ok, but visible abs aren't.

Men

Back Day: 500 reps

Lats: Start with cable pullovers, barbell pulldowns and pull-ups. Then, perform high rows, mid rows and low rows on the T-bar. Finish with long rows. Podium: Perform barbell and bodyweight hyperextensions. Train neck last. Do 50 reps of each exercise.

Chest Day: 500 reps

Chest: Start with the incline bench press first, dumbbell flat bench press second and the decline bench press last. Each exercise requires 50 reps. After that, do 100 reps of cable cross pec flies. Abs: Do 50 reps on a fully-jacked ab bench with a barbell, 100 bodyweight reps on a fully-jacked ab bench and finish with 100 kicks on the joysticks.

Trap Day: 500 reps

Start off with cable and smith machine shrugs. Next, use dumbbells for reverse flyes on your middle and lower traps. Finish with around the worlds. Do 100 reps of each.

Arm Day: 500 reps

Triceps: Start with barbell skull crushers for 50 reps. Next, hit dumbbell French curls for 50 reps. After that, lay down and perform cross-body kickbacks for 100 reps with dumbbells. Biceps: Start with e-z bar preacher curls first, then move on to dumbbell hammer curls, blast reverse barbell curls third and finish with Zottman curls. All four exercises require 25 reps. Forearms: Perform 100 wrist curls and 100 dumbbell twirls.

Legs: 500 reps

Start with front squats on the power squat and Romanian deadlifts. Use light weight and perform the reps slowly. Then, hit barbell calf press, hip machine for the inner hips and cable crossover for the outer hips. Each exercise requires 100 reps. If you're not capable of squatting, here's a list of other exercises in order of difficulty: smith machine squat > hack squat > power squat > hip sled > incline leg press > leg press.

Shoulder Day: 500 reps

Perform overhead press on the power squat machine. Then, perform upright rows in the squat rack and use the foam-padded side delt machine. Finish with rear delt pullups on the assisted pullup and cable lat pulldowns. *Each exercise needs 100 reps.*

Cardio Day: 45 minutes

Start with the treadmill and work on building speed, not incline. Sprint occasionally until you have 15 minutes of sprinting underneath your belt not counting your rest intervals. Then, nail 15 minutes on the Stairmaster with max resistance to toast your glutes. Finally, cycle for 15 minutes to loosen up your hamstrings. Now, stretch your hamstrings and hips on the stretch cage for 15 minutes before heading on home.

Review

Performance

Supplementation:

Most vitamins and supplements are unnecessary for you to take. Multivitamins are for healthy people with terrible diets. Individual vitamins are for people who've been diagnosed with medical deficiencies in one type of vitamin. Glutamine is for marathon runners trying to prevent their legs from overtraining. Creatine helps injured people work out. Weight gainer gives starving people a chance to recover. Fat burner is for fat people. Pre-workout should be reserved for PRs. Protein powder benefits people who cannot achieve the daily value of protein due to money reasons.

Injuries

Hip Joints:

Do you know why old people have problems with their hips? It's because they never trained their hip flexors! People will make fun of you for doing these exercises. Yet, you're not the one who will have osteoporosis and you'll have strong hip joints until the day you die. You'll squat more and may even be able to kick several hundred pounds into the air. Not only can you kick the crap out of someone, you're stronger than them since everything is in the legs! You won't have some retarded-looking buttocks. Most of them only train upper-body. Have you seen these guys? Their butts look like two Reese's peanut butter cups with two side pits. That's not natural, guys!

Steroid-Free:

Naturals at 200 lbs.+ with 4% fat will have a chance to become some of the World's strongest men. You have men who are 450 lbs. that can't even lift a fraction of what Eugen Sandown did during the late 1800s at 205 lbs. If they have cut marks near their nipples, gynecomastia and look fat with visible abs, then there's a possibility that they're drug users. Being overly musclebound not only looks terrible, it slows you down and is unhealthy for your body to maintain over time. Guys, stay drug free!

CHAPTER THREE

Proper Penmanship

Overview

Competency

Your Resources:

Proper Penmanship discusses appropriate business wardrobes, writing techniques and college strategies. There are certain paper colors, page quantities and pen colors you're supposed to use when creating reports. Mechanical pencils are for inventory ledgers in log books, flat pencils are for carpentry purposes and No. 2 pencils are for college students. All of these things matter! Cream paper is used in legal documents and white paper by businesses or for academic reasons. That was several examples.

Professionalism:

You'll need to know how to impress the interviewer, make a résumé correctly, create nice letters of recommendation and generate high-quality thank you letters. Good posture, solid eye contact and firm, dry handshakes show people you're the one and they're not. Show them how to dress like a man or woman instead of dressing like a wimpy bum. Turning your head to the side and looking down is acceptable while thinking of past events. However, everything else in discussion requires eye contact.

Education

College Burnouts:

Natives must avoid making the same mistakes the Anglo-Saxons make. You need to become employed, gain work experience and gather necessary resources to further your education. Now, you no longer have to complain about tuition or book costs. You'll already understand the criteria and place into higher levels of management compared to other graduates. Most of the time, they'll just get a basic skilled position or internship. You, on the other hand, shall place into the next managerial position up. Each degree marks another ten years of your age. Anglos don't understand this: 20+ starting associates, 30+ starting bachelors, 40+ starting masters and 50+ starting doctoral degrees. Avoid their mistakes and the cramming that causes burnouts.

Employment

Résumé

Title Page:

The title page proceeds the cover page. It displays a full-title listing the presentation's name at the top, a color picture called a frontispiece in the middle and the author's full name at the bottom. Title pages on résumés, reports and books are multi-spaced.

Cover Page:

Cover pages list what you're applying for, which location you wish to work at, why you've applied for the position and what motivated you to do so. It also lists when you can start and how to reach you. Add a salutation and a full signature in blue pen.

Experience Page:

This should be a page long displaying your work experiences, dates of employment and managerial contact information. List why you left employment from previous occupations. Tailor it to list the best positions that apply to the job you'll occupy. List two pages for middle-management and three pages for the upper-management jobs.

Education Page:

List your education first, your extracurricular activities or veteran status next and any references for them to contact at the very bottom. Never go beyond a page in length.

Thanks Page:

Be sure to include a thank you so you don't have to follow up with an email. Use a salutation followed by your handwritten initials always signed in blue. If you really want to go the distance, follow up with a thank you letter in the form of a nice email.

Recommendations:

Applicants don't write these. Print a color copy on glossy paper. Modern letters of recommendation are usually emailed. If you write them by hand, write the body in black and sign your full signature at the bottom in blue. It's highly unlikely that they would ever be written on cream paper. If so, write and sign them with a black pen.

Postscripts:

Teachers use red pens for grading/criticism, blue pens for adding credit/critiques and black pens if handwriting letters. Sign job applications or receipts with blue pens.

Wardrobe

Entrance Foyers:

Foyers have two sets of double doors because they're checkpoints for guests. They give them a place to set down their coats, hats, canes and umbrellas before entering.

Formal Wear (Bowtie):

Tuxedoes aren't formal white-tie attire; they're semi-formal black tie! Wear top hats, cravats, tailcoats with shawl lapels, double-breasted dress coats, suspenders, patent leather belts/shoes and white bowties. Semi-formal events favor men in black suits, cummerbunds, peaked lapel jackets, tuxedo shirts/socks/shoes and black bowties.

Suits (Necktie):

Informal business suits are for offices. During colder seasons, wear fedoras, neckties, dress shirts, overcoats, suit jackets with notch lapels, dress belts, dress socks and dress shoes. For warmer seasons, wear bowler hats, western neckties, dress shirts with the sleeves rolled up, topcoats, vests with notched lapels, pocket watches and dress belts. For business casual during colder seasons, wear Homburg hats, blazers and slacks. During your warmer seasons, wear pork pie hats and Kentucky neckties.

Cowboy Attire:

Wear this for ranching duties. During colder seasons, wear felt cowboy hats, bolo neckties, flannel shirts and fringe jackets. During the warmer seasons, wear straw cowboy hats, bandanas, western shirts and leather vests. Wear western belts, spurs, cowboy hats and cowboy boots. Ditch cowboy hats, tail coats and chaps at the foyers.

Casual Wear:

Street attire: For colder times, wear sock caps, long-sleeved tucked-in shirts, leather jackets, corduroy pants, leather belts, wool socks and loafers. For warmer seasons, wear flat caps, short-sleeved untucked shirts, V-neck sweaters, casual belts, crew socks and boots. Wear crew neck undershirts. Scarfs and turtlenecks are for women.

Sporting Attire:

For sporting needs. During colder seasons, wear hoodies, long-sleeved shirts, sweat pants and tube socks. For warmer seasons, wear baseball caps, short-sleeved shirts, shorts and athletic socks. Sportswear get briefs and running shoes while everything else has boxers. In gyms, wear tank tops if you're in shape. Sport coats are for polo.

Work Clothes:

Rain coats, boots and bucket hats are for fishermen. Skipper hats are for saltwater boat captains. Overalls are for farmers and coveralls are for painters. Lab coats are removed after leaving laboratories. Chefs wear toques and cooks don forage caps.

Presentation Sizes

1. Primary School:

A. under 250 words.

B. ½ page review.

2. Middle School:

A. 250-500 words.

B. 1 page abstract.

3. Secondary School:

A. 500-750 words.

B. 2-3 page report.

4. Associates Courses:

A. 750-1,500 words.

B. 3-6 page essay.

5. Bachelors Courses:

A. 1,500-3,000 words.

B. 6-12 page term.

6. Masters Courses:

A. 3,000-6,000 words.

B. 12-24 page thesis.

7. Doctoral Exams:

A. 6,000-12,000 words.

B. 24-48 page dissertation.

8. Principal Investigator:

A. 12,000-30,000 words.

B. 48-130 page handbook.

Creation:

Review: Reviews involve writing what you think about a book.

Abstract: Abstracts involve learning how to write intro pages.

Report: A report includes writing a summary and critique.

Essay: Essays involve typing up arguments over a said plan.

Term: Terms involve typing up arguments about a said field.

Thesis: A thesis showcases field mastery and advancement.

Dissertation: Dissertations are future changes to a field.

Handbook: Handbooks sets new industry standards.

Review

Effectiveness

Legal Fortification:

Make sure your legal documents (articles) are no longer than 48 pages and are always printed on cream paper. Use a preamble (intro), table of authorities, amendment title pages listing sections and an appendix indexing its various annexes. Annexes are subsections of an appendix, often listing charts. Codicils are parts of a will, trust or estate. Present documents with a paperclip inside a folder. Never fold or staple them.

Employment Experience:

Make sure that every time you make a business transaction to have legally-certified documentation, and witnesses you know and trust present. The nonnatives are crooked and careless. When they sign with you, they're called notaries notarizing things. Whenever you set a price, always calculate every fixed cost. Set a flat-rate fee for your services. Divide the total fee by the number of hours you've already worked. This number should be comparable to the equivalent hourly wage for your position.

Allocation

Truth and Fairness:

Always undercut the competition's price by a third and portion size by 10%. Anything more than that could cause you to lose money and anything less may not steal their customers away. Make sure your children's personal lives and business dealings are just like yours: truly honest and fair. Furthermore, make sure they don't show any animosity towards their opponents until they're defeated. Don't get mad; get even!

Making Payments:

Don't pay anyone in the higher positions of your company an hourly wage. They'll receive a percentage per job or year. They're contract labor with 1099 commissions. Use salaries for management. Grunts are given hourly wages with W2 tax forms.

CHAPTER FOUR

Proper Transportation

Overview

Transportation

Mandatory Muscle:

Chapter Four reveals how to design quality vehicles for your transportation needs. Aluminum bodies are cheaper than fiberglass and can be recycled at salvage yards. Variable displacement lets engines shut off half of their cylinders whenever they're idling or cruising to double their fuel economy. Combining this feature with a hybrid electric powerplant could quadruple one's gas mileage! A smaller, supercharged gas engine or turbocharged diesel requires less petrol and maintenance too. Proper exhaust allows any motor to generate a low-pitched growl without killing efficiency.

Logistical Independence:

The next generation of natives advancing into the towns need to understand how to operate railroad switches and cutoffs. This gives natives the ability to slowly absorb the competition's railroads. Building lines in mountain valleys reduces dependence on trucking, which drives the prices of goods down. Watercraft convert the water beneath their hulls into hydrogen, giving them an infinite fuel source. With less demand for fossil fuels, our national petroleum reserves can stockpile the excess!

Refueling

Competitive Edge:

Smaller gas stations cost less to operate, thus allowing small businesses to match the prices of larger corporations. Petrol gets stale the longer it sits. Always power wash your concrete and repaint whenever necessary. Otherwise, customers feel like they've entered a dangerous neighborhood. A 24-hour location accepting food stamps always holds the greatest advantage over its competitors. Plus is mixed onsite by blending regular and premium gasoline together. You can offer all three at every terminal, but don't stock too much. However, diesel is only available at a few pumps. Place all terminals out-front and connect them to the store by an awning.

Automobile Engines

Compact Cars

Daimler Phoenix I4s:

Inline fours are the most economical. Most boxer engines are placed in the rear of Porches and VW Beetles. V4s are popular in inland boats. Larger motorcycle designs utilized them, but charged twin-cams render them obsolete. Supercharged varieties give jeeps more torque to haul trailers and sedans horsepower during acceleration.

Marmon Wasp V6s:

Suburban utility vehicles and larger jeeps ditch their V8s for a supercharged, 3.5L V6. SUVs are weighed-down by passengers and jeeps need enough torque to tow trailers. Minivans replaced most station wagons, but both should utilize this engine design. Subaru continues to produce these designs for those desiring to tow objects on top of the vehicle while providing adequate capacity to passengers. In order for passenger vans to compete with them, they've been beefed-up to assume more industrial duties. Therefore, their V6s shall be replaced with turbocharged diesels.

Antoinettes

Small Block V8s:

NASCAR relies on naturally-aspirated stock cars. As the rules changed, carburetors were replaced with fuel injection. Ironically, it's not about one's top speed. Instead, reducing pitting to perform maintenance or refueling is key. All vehicles must have a small block V8 ($\leq$ 5.9L) with a high-compression tuning and restrictor plate on air intakes. Quarter-ton trucks and new muscle cars don supercharged, 4.5L versions! All American sports, luxury sports and super cars are designated two-seater coupés.

Big Block V8s:

Generally defined as 6.5L or greater, there exists three major purposes for these monstrosities. A properly-rated half-ton truck shouldn't be limited to a 6L engine. Instead, give them 6.5L fuel-injected and suspensions capable of hauling 1,000 lbs. within their beds. Funny cars are front-engine dragsters capable of pulling wheelies. Regulations prohibit anything beyond an 8L running ethanol. Monster trucks burn methanol in their 9.5L monstrosities. Give the latter two dual, four-barreled carbs, blowers and nitrous oxide (NOS). All three come standard with one supercharger.

Mid-engines

Alpha Romeo V10s:

Supercars are divided into two categories: Muscle and hypercars. The latter are almost exclusively mid-engine (rear engine) vehicles with at least 10 cylinders. Installing a twin-supercharged, 5.5L V10 with fuel rails guarantees the best balance between horsepower (top speed), torque (takeoff) and growl (low-pitched sounds).

Formula One V12s:

Formula One racing placed restrictions forcing turbocharged, 1.5L V6 engines on racers. They believe this reduces cost, but engines only last one or two races and sound like bumblebees trapped in empty beer cans! Fans are losing interest in this sport because of this. We should encourage them to return to the days of 5L V12s by Ferrari. In fact, let's give them twin superchargers and fuel rails to push 1,500 hp! All problems can be solved by installing governors on top of their RPM limiters.

The Cadillac V16s:

Drag rails follow the same restrictions as funny cars do when it comes to their 8L limitations. What separates them from the rest is the fact most designs are mid-engine. Therefore, a twin-supercharged V16 engine is not considered overkill. Some run ethanol while others, methanol. Twin fuel rails and NOS canisters are required.

Diesels

Inline Fours:

There have been highly-successful 3-cylinder cargo trucks and 5-cylinder cars put in to commission. Unfortunately, odd-numbered engines aren't ideal. Pairing straight threes together constructs V6s, fours build V8s, fives make V10s and sixes V12s. I recommend supplanting passenger vans' V6s with twin-turbocharged inline fours. The smaller charger is for low gear while the bigger one takes over at higher speeds.

Straight Sixes:

Semis and dump trucks are powered by turbocharged straight sixes. Exhaust is split in to two vertical stacks, yet engines aren't V10s or greater. That's why they follow the same twin-turbo layout as inline fours do. Quad-turbos are for heavy industrial vehicles and octuple-turbo blocks on prime movers of freight forwarding agencies.

Dually V8s:

The dually achieves greater acceleration than its counterparts due to its V-shaped block. Yet, it doesn't pull as much torque as the other three options do. A lack in towing capacity is negated by its better fuel economy and automatic transmission.

Forwarding Cargo

Construction

Timber Yarder Towers:

Yarders are offroad vehicles that are essentially small cranes developed for timber companies operating on mountains. The largest rarely exceed 80 short tons. Give them quad-turbocharged, V10s. Much like the other biodiesel engine blocks below, fuel economy is improved by two things: Hybrid electric motors while idling and variable displacement during top-gear cruising, which shuts down half the cylinders!

Bulldozer Crawlers:

Crawlers are treaded tractor cabs, lack tires and drive front buckets called dozers. Bulldozers combine both roles together. Anything under 200 tons can avoid having a pair of twin-eights for quad-turbo V12s. Graders and scrapers travel on 4x4 tires.

Hydraulic Excavators:

Vehicles over 1,000 tons only need one octuple-turbocharged, hybrid electric, V16 with variable displacement. Larger diggers demand continuous "tank" tracks while our smaller backhoe models are issued current industry-standard, run-flat 4x4 tires.

Freighting

Hauling Trucks:

For ultra class cabs deployed in quarries, a V18 with eight turbos outperforms a pair of twin-turbo V16s or quad-turbo V20! Historically, most rear-eject bodies had three axles. Future models resemble dual-axle, end-dump vehicles catering to sticky payloads ensuring a 100% offload. Tailgates can move just like their articulators do!

NASA Transporters:

A pair of turbocharged V18s powered the original shuttle crawlers to their launch sites at poor speeds of 1-2 mph. Retrofitting an octuple-turbocharged, hybrid electric, V18 with variable displacement lets each vehicle travel several times faster!

Freight Trains:

It's not uncommon for passenger lines to push 1k tons and freight routes 10k tons, but freight railways can reach 100k tons! A locomotive housing an octuple-turbocharged, hybrid electric, V20 with variable displacement should do the trick!

Hydrogen Watercraft

Powerplants

H20 Engine Blocks:

Beneath each watercraft lies a pump powered by gravity and forward osmosis. Its purpose is to refill the water tank. Molecules are separated into hydrogen, oxygen and salt by electrolysis. Gases are stored inside compressed air tanks and pumped through well-insulated air hoses. This grants mariners the opportunity to enjoy a cigarette without posing as a potential fire hazard or initiating massive explosions.

Hydrogen Hybrids:

Boaters benefit from my fuel-injected, internal combustion engines with variable displacement and hybrid electric motors. Top fuel racers opt for dual, four-barrel carburetors with blowers. Apart from river ferries receiving twin turbochargers firing in intervals, give all inland watercraft and coastal speedboats superchargers!

Boilers and Turbines:

Hydrogen-fired boilers and steam turbines supplant diesel engines and gas turbines in ships and saltwater boats. Refrigerated fuel tanks in engine rooms generate all the power they need, so don't bother giving them piston-driven blocks! Nuclear warships convert sodium chloride into molten sea salt inside their thorium reactors.

Littorals

Offshore V16s:

All-weather USCG lifeboats and civilian yachts are 50'-80' vessels displacing 20-50 tons. Mounting a single twin-supercharged, 7.5L, V16 inboard should do the trick!

Nearshore V12s:

Fairweather USCG lifeboats and saltwater-capable speedboats often range 40'-50' in length. Unlike inflatable designs, aluminum hulls can easily displace around 10-20 tons when fully-loaded. Run a twin-supercharged, 6.5L, V12 inboard engine block.

Inshore V10s:

Inshore lifeboats and saltwater fishing boats are at least 25'-40' in length and rarely exceed 4-10 tons when fully-loaded. Install a twin-supercharged, 5.5L, V10 inboard.

Inboards

Top Fuel Racing:

Drag races can achieve 300+ mph in 3 or more seconds. Regardless of fuel source, one thing remains the same: An 8L, supercharged, blower-fed, dual-carbureted V8! Unlike other blocks, they do not require variable drive or hybrid electric efficiency.

Transport Ferries:

Salters and lakers are powered by hydrogen boilers and steam turbines. Oversized river ferries displace 100-250 tons and demand twin-turbocharged, 9.5L V8s. Mid-sized variants displacing 50-100 tons only require 8L versions. The smallest options averaging 20-50 tons still need 6.5L big blocks. Bigger cylinders and turbochargers generate more torque, which enhances towing capacity. Since they're not involved in completive racing, there's no need for high-performance carburetors. Electronic fuel injection systems offer superior fuel economy and further reduce maintenance.

Waterfront Police:

Local police forces patrol inland lakes and rivers. They must perform high-speed rescue missions with supercharged, 4.5L, small block V8s! Fuel injection systems blend the perfect balance between outright performance and financial economy. Missions range from interceptions to SAR (search and rescue). Hybrid electrics kick in during idling while variable displacement furthers fuel economy as flotillas cruise.

Jet-propelled Skiing:

Jet-boats are rarely no more than 35' in length. Tubers and skiing enthusiasts are shieled from their propellors by tucking them within internal bays, which provide jet propulsion. These blocks shouldn't exceed the power output of a supercharged, 3.5L V6. Their lightweight, fiberglass hulls reduce weight and improve performance.

Rotary PWCs:

Kawasaki holds the trademark to the term Jet Ski. Everyone else must refer to their creation as a personal water craft (PWC). Limit supercharged Wankel blocks to 1.5L.

Outboards

Pontoon Boats:

A supercharged, fuel-injected,.3.5L V6 provides plenty of power to even the biggest pontoon boats! These designs lack hybrid electric motors, but have cylinder shutoff.

Bass Fishermen:

Supercharging an outboard, 2.5L 4-cylinder is more than plenty for an average bass boat. They also lack hybrid electric features, but do possess variable displacement.

Review

Reservoirs

Deepwater Drilling:

Some beaches depend on tourism. To preserve their beauty, they prohibit offshore drilling. Underwater "snake lines" grant deepwater oil rigs access to these coastal deposits. Doing so can further reduce the number of existing drilling platforms too.

Underground Lifelines:

Buried pipelines are protected and less unsightly. Your mechanical failsafe systems isolate damaged sections to prevent water aquafers from becoming contaminated.

Refueling

Parks & Wildlife:

State parks are organized into three tiers of divisions. Checkpoints are manned by deputies and receive one service pump. Ranger outposts have a second terminal for civilian boaters unloading watercraft at marinas. Headquarters bases led by game wardens also have a third pump stocked with jet fuel to service patrol helicopters.

Filling Stations:

My definition of what local incorporations is different than that of today's society. Small, commuter townships (3A) should have at least four, 4-pump stations. Market towns (4A) necessitate four, 8-pump service centers. Larger satellites (5A) demand four, 16-pump depots. The latter category sometimes serves as a "de facto" city in the absence of a micropolis (16k-64k). These anchors make one to a truck stop. Give micros 16 centers, metropolises (64k-256k) 64 and megalopolises (256k-1mil+) 256!

Truck Stops:

Micros have up to four districts and need one rest stop. Metros are four divisions. Therefore, there are 16 districts and four truck stops. Megas are organized into four or more boroughs. This means 64 districts, 16 urban divisions and 16 truck stops!

CHAPTER FIVE

Plantation Strategies

Overview

Shires

Headquarters:

Plantation Strategies discusses the first generation's business plan and the first major offensive of the natives. You need to take over all of the land outside of every town and city in the country first. You'll need to stop the nonnatives from being able to bring in more non-Hispanic immigrants or breeding an even larger nonnative population. This halts their advance forever and allows the second generation, your children, a chance to infiltrate the said towns and take over their pink-collar industry!

Farm Research:

Before doing anything, find out if you can mine or drill on your farming plot. Second, find out what can grow in your area. If you can't grow your region's crops on your land, see what animals can thrive in your region. If you can't raise their animals, then you're on mountains or in a xeric area. In this case, follow my mountain animals list. They're not just for mountains, they're for xeric areas in flatter terrains also. Once you find out what your region can raise and discover if you have the makings for a plantation or a ranch, check what type of town or city you're outside of. There are six different-sized ranches and six different-sized plantations for these six farming areas.

Families

Unsubsidized:

The large, unsubsidized family farm shall represent the future upper class of Native American society. Largeholding plantations are above 50 acres, and orbit town or city loops. Estates are 400+ acres, span the highways or farm-to-markets, and some are agricultural plantations. Each plantation contains two crop fields. Fields split into meadows, and those funnel into patches. All Native American ranches shall undercut nonnatives' factory farm prices with the "double-grazing" method. 100% organic farms avoid using pesticides, fertilizers and GMOs (genetically-modified organisms).

38

Sustainable Plantations

The West

West Coast:

Washington is known for its apple production. Oregon has underrated park systems. Idaho is famous for its potatoes. Cold conifers in the mountains support their sawmills. The California Valley produces most of the West Coast's milk, grapes and wine. Their xeric mountain ranges sustain mining. There are rich oil deposits offshore. Hawaiian mountains' climate and soil are capable of sustaining tropical fruit farming.

The Rockies:

Drier mountain ranges can support mining and timber production of xeric conifers. The valleys near the border of Arizona and New Mexico always yield agave, aloe vera, medicinal cacti, medicinal herbs and dark honey made from cacti. Their marshes can aid in wild rice production. Taiga mountain ranges benefit timber production of colder conifers. Mountain springs can be used to supply future beverage companies.

Central

First up, is the Great Plains. The warmer region is known as Tornado Alley. It sustains corn, wheat, barley, hops, grains, cereals and various breads. Its colder region (underground supervolcano) is known as the Empty Quarter. It supports sorghum, hay, wheat, barley and beet production. The Dakotas have mountains suited towards timber production of cold conifer species. Their badlands support mining also. You should be able to garner stone countertops and tile flooring from your mining efforts.

The East

The Great Lakes are perfect for beverages, cranberries, dairy products and timber. Appalachia is a great area for hardwood timber, coal mining, stone mining and tobacco production. Northern Appalachia is known for blueberries, maple timber, maple syrup, fruit, hazelnuts and walnut plantations. Our southern flatwoods area yields cotton, pecans and night crawlers from their catalpa trees. Florida and Puerto Rico are great for rice, citrus and avocados. They also can grow tropical fruits and supply tropical hardwoods. Just like Hawaii, they can have palm plantations too!

Unsubsidized Plantations

Largeholdings

Agricultural Estates:

If fertility supports crops outside towns instead of just ranching, open textile mills. For towns, $\leq$ 3As tackle cotton production; 4As raise flax for linen and 5As cultivate American silk moths to create brown silk. Select regional hardwoods, according to *Saving the United States*, for them to feed on. Cannabis is covered in my sixth book, *Cannabis Market*. There are three plot sizes for industrial fiber (50 acres), edible grain (100 acres) and CBD-rich (200 acres) hemp. Marijuana follows suit, but has smallholdings with sativa (25 acres), balanced hybrids (10 acres) and indica (5 acres).

Homestead Plantations:

Homesteads outside towns' shires focus on starches. Sizes range from 2,000 acres (grains) in commuters, 1,000 acres (legumes) in market towns and 500 acres (tubers) in satellites. Buried drip lines serve as irrigation. Farms in city parishes are 200 acres (mushrooms), 100 acres (greens) and 50 acres (berries). All three get micro sprinklers.

Compounds

Hydroponic Labs:

Urban farms set aside indoor grow labs to vertically farm smaller crops using tower gardens (poles with planting holes). A half-acre germinates, an acre strengthens seedlings and two acres handle adults. Larger species grow outdoors. Aeroponics uses ultrasonic foggers, low-pressure units and high-pressure commercial machines for micro greens. Active hydroponics has shallow water cultures (SWCs), nutrient film technique (NFT) and drip lines. Passive hydroponics includes Ebb & Flow, Kratky Method and Wick Method. Various-sized hydroton (clay pebbles) are their mediums.

Private Roadways:

Within plantations, rock roads link farm hubs to fields. Pea gravel routes join fields to their meadows allowing go-karts access. Irrigation is monitored via the use of POS systems, a type of specially-designed computer software program, run through laptops. Wooden plank roads link these areas to crop patches. Each patch has multiple dirt trails serving as walkways called service aisles. Several crop rows are visible to those traveling down them. Plumbing closets are concealed within huts.

Timber Plantations

Park systems are co-ops of private parks reporting to a deputy ranger. They lease plots up to 5,000 acres in size within the preserves to loggers. The majority of land usage on plots are set aside for pine barrens. All timber is naturally-rated because it uses plant-based insect repellants, sealants and wood treatment.

Blonde Furniture

1. **Ash:** Indoor Furniture
2. **Basswood:** Blinds, Fans
3. **Birch:** Interior Plywood
4. **Boxelder:** Boxes, Crates
5. **Butternut:** Kitchen Cabinets
6. **Chestnut:** Beds, Desks
7. **Hickory:** Culinary Gear
8. **Poplar:** Beds' Framing
9. **Quaking Aspen:** Faggots
10. **White Oak:** Minor Cabinets
11. **Willow:** Patio Furniture

Dark Furniture

1. **Black Oak:** Minor Cabinets
2. **Cherry:** Indoor Furniture
3. **Hackberry:** Dashboards
4. **Locust:** Doors, Stair Cases
5. **Mahogany:** Beds, Desks
6. **Manzanita:** Dark Faggots
7. **Maple:** Floors, Front Doors
8. **Mesquite:** Wall Paneling
9. **Teak:** Boat Decks/Wheels
10. **Tupelo:** Patio Furniture
11. **Walnut:** Kitchen Cabinets

Exteriors

1. **Cedar:** Patio Decking
2. **Cypress:** Bulkheads
3. **Fir:** Particle Board
4. **Hemlock:** Powerlines
5. **Juniper:** Fence Boards
6. **Larch:** Watersports
7. **Pine:** Interior Framing
8. **Spruce:** New Paper
9. **Yew:** Roof Overhangs

Tools

1. **Apple:** Bacon Smoking
2. **Beech:** Beer Production
3. **Birch:** Syrup Production
4. **Elms:** Broom Handles
5. **Hickory:** BBQ, Baking
6. **Hornbeam:** Hammers
7. **Hophornbeam:** Posts
8. **Maple:** Syrup Trees
9. **Sassafras:** Drinks

Review

Setups

Farm Loans:

For farm financing, only use the farmers' credit unions. They can offer you 40-year mortgages down to 10-year loans or less. They offer non-compounding interest rates too! Instead of adding on to each month's principal payment, they add to the entire mortgage's principal value. If you borrowed $1 million, don't expect to pay anything above $1.2 million. If you borrowed that from a bank, you could very easily see a grand total of at least $4 million. Also, the unions won't penalize you for early payoffs.

Farm Expansion:

When expanding your farm, follow these three steps in chronological order: First, buy younger product to save money and breed them once they're older. Ducks can help eat pests off of your crops, but will require beak dipping stations or pools. If you don't give the ducks adequate dipping stations, they'll develop a dark crust around their eyes that causes blindness. You can go organic, but give timber the lower "natural" rating. After all, the timber is sprayed with treatment to seal it. Second, buy more land when you have the funds. Third, replace old fleets of used equipment with larger fleets of newer gear. These expenses serve as tax deductions on your tax returns. All farms will have windmill electricity, propane heating, well water and septic systems.

COOPs

The Fleets:

First, buy a used tractor and join a co-op. Each neighbor has a different type of tractor in the co-op. One neighbor bails everyone's hay while another tills everyone's farm. Next, buy a small fleet of used tractors. After that, replace it with a large fleet of new ones. Start out with metal sheds, trailers and fences. Then, upgrade to wooden ones. Farmers and butchers don't compete; they just put someone else's company sticker on it. The catch is that farmers forfeit the right to operate their own retail store.

CHAPTER SIX

Ranching Strategies

Overview

Startup

Geography:

First, find out what region you are in. If you can mine or drill, go for it! If not, here's a list detailing what animals will do well in your area and what products the regional markets desire most. Second, use the directions listed in the previous chapter's review about financing, partnering and fleet establishment. Find out which city or town you're in and raise the animals I've listed for that type of plot. If you're in a xeric mountain range, you might have to raise mountain animals indigenous to the area.

Grazing

Double-Grazing:

There are two things you must understand about ranches: The three different types of plots for the three different kinds of cities won't use the double-grazing method. That's because they don't stock any hooved animals with their poultry. Second, the three different types of plots for the three different kinds of towns do use the double-grazing method. This involves cycling pastures where the hooved animals tip the tall grass down to a medium height. Then, poultry are sent in and cause the medium-height grass to become short. Lastly, the shortened grass receives seasonal burning and is left to heal. During that time, you apply aged manure into your fields.

Faster Rotations:

Your goal is to only take the tips off the grass while grazing. The grass takes a day or two to grow back. Most people let a small handful of animals continually munch on a large pasture's grass for more than a day. Instead, constantly move a large herd on a small pasture for one day. If your livestock are spoiled from only eating tips, they'll avoid overgrazing grass that's already been tipped. Constantly herd your livestock in your pastures to prevent them from overgrazing certain areas. Once the pen's pasture reaches a certain height, move your herds into the other pastures.

Sustainable Ranching

Great Lakes

The Great Lakes is famous for its dairy production. Forested areas around the lakes are known for their cold winters and sandy soil in their pine barrens. Any time you have a dairy farm, you're going to have veal production also. This region will have the country's largest veal production rivaled only by California. Ranches, on the other hand, usually turn their male calves into steers. That's why ranches produce less veal.

Northeast

Northeastern lands are true poultry strongholds. Their flatwoods areas have similar climates and plant life. Turkey, chicken and quail are major products from the region. When raising pheasant and ducks, use the flightless breeds. Ducks need to have a pond or a dipping station for dietary, health and sanitation reasons. If ducks can't wet their eyes, they'll develop blindness. The best way to set up a duck farm is to open one next to a natural pond or marsh. This prevents you from having to reroute water from watersheds, draining water tables or creating water shortages during droughts.

Deep South

The South is well known for two things: BBQ pork along Appalachia's eastern coast and cattle ranches along the Gulf Coast. In the Central Flatwoods, poultry is a huge staple. Poultry includes turkey, chicken, quail, pheasant and duck. (Fowl are the wild versions.) Follow the rules listed earlier in this chapter while managing poultry. You'll have to prevent mite infestations and any eye conditions caused by dry eyes.

Western Valleys

The valleys of the Southwest may have been oak flatwoods. There may have been a possibility of having both prairies and flatwoods in the valleys at the same time depending upon the terrain, watersheds and fall lines. If you're in a flatwoods area, run cattle. If it's a prairie area, run plantations. Prairies are more fertile than pine barrens. Goat milk, goat meat, lamb and sheep's wool are products that should be reared in dry mountains. They prevent overgrazing and are excellent during droughts or grazing rough terrain. (*California uses the most water from the Hoover dam!*)

Sustainable Aquaculture

Fishing

The Northwest is known for its salmon, halibut and bottomfish. New England is a stronghold for cold-water Maine lobster. (the only species that has the claws) Spiny lobsters have the antennae arms and grow around the subtropical regions. The Mississippi and Gulf wetlands are known for catfish, crayfish, shrimp, frog's legs and alligator. No freshwater area in the U.S. sells as much fish as this bottomland region!

Shellfish

Production:

Almost every coastal area has the same thing: clams, oysters, scallops and mussels. Check to see what's native to your region. Abalone are sea snails along the West Coast. Only harvest and consume during months with the letter "R" in their names.

Jewelry:

Use mother-of-pearl in tea sets, china and electric guitar inlays. For pearl production, carefully insert a grain of sand as an irritant into either a mussel or an oyster. If you don't do this right, the pearl won't form correctly and could actually kill the shellfish.

Fisheries:

If you raise fish and release them back into the wild, they count as wild-caught once fishermen catch them again. This increases their value and gives them better flavor.

Aquaponics

Only setup major hydroponics hubs in areas with enough water to sustain them, such as the Great Lakes. Plants can serve as floral arrangements, food, herbs and medicine. Only use native plants to prevent future invasive species outbreaks. In the ocean, edible plants like seaweed are popular in Japanese dishes. We can keep their species secure through the use of aquaponics. Biofuel blends work excellent in diesel, while ethanol works wonders in gasoline. Both additives increase fuel mileage, horsepower and torque. They'll have a better color and aroma, while being less toxic or noxious. Mix 10% ethanol into gasoline and 14% biodiesel additives into your diesel mixtures.

Unsubsidized Ranching

Plot Sizes

A. Megalopolitan: 50 acres

B. Metropolitan: 100 acres

C. Micropolitan: 200 acres

D. Satellite Town: 400 acres

E. Market Town: 1,000 acres

F. Commuter Town: 2,000 acres

Asset Goals

A. Land: $1 million

B. Equipment: $1 million

C. Crops/Livestock: $1 million

D. Gross Sales: $500k annually

E. Net Profit: $20k annually

F. Farm Type: Organic Rating

Grass-Fed

A. Pastured Hogs: 400 acres

B. Sheep Herding: 1,000 acres

C. Bison/Cattle: 2,000 acres

Pastured

A. Chicken Farm: 400 acres

B. Duck Farm: 1,000 acres

C. Turkey Farm: 2,000 acres

Free-Range

A. Rabbit Farm: 50 acres

B. Pheasant Farm: 100 acres

C. Quail Farm: 200 acres

Food Sources

A. Grass-Fed: entirely plants

B. Pastured: mostly from plants

C. Free-Range: mostly feed

Organic Ranches

Beehives need 8,000 acres between other hives, bovine animals need four acres and horses need two acres per head. Limit four sheep, 10 hogs, 20 turkeys, 40 ducks, 80 chickens, 1,000 pheasants, 2,000 quails or 4,000 rabbits per acre. Graze the grass-fed animals first and then the pastured poultry next. Burn every 90 days and cycle all pastures. Use non-GMO plant-based herbs, never antibiotics!

Review

Towns

Double Strike:

Native largeholdings, aka homesteads, focus on joining co-ops and farmer's markets. Larger farms outside of the towns, aka estates, tackle the corporate farms with their double-grazing method. Some estates give jobs to people who can't afford to buy their own farm. They can sell their used equipment to them once it's depreciated. This turns smallholdings, once only capable of being a hobby farm, to go professional!

The Townships:

Second generation natives take the towns' jobs away from the nonnatives. They'll use their funds to open businesses mimicking their rivals. The goal is to work "top-down". If you crush a mill, then the nearby culinary establishments could fall without you even having to do anything. If that fails, work your way down to the menial ones. Even though the nonnatives outnumber you, business owners only represent two to five percent of your country. Therefore, most of the nonnatives are just employees.

Cities

The "Polis":

The second generation from the estates outside of the cities have two options: First, reinforce the urban homesteads to accelerate the takeover of urban farmland. After that, idle forces can start to use the book's urban quadrant to open factories in the cities and crush the nonnatives' factories. This gives the third-generation natives a head start. Remember: Always hire natives first, Hispanics next and nonnatives last.

The "Tans":

City limits around the world, especially in Europe, have farms outside of their limits. It's not supposed to be more suburbs! Their homesteads will serve as the natives' frontlines and prevent cities from sprawling into minor anchors or nearby towns.

CHAPTER SEVEN

Resource Management

Overview

Energy

Management:

There's no miraculously infinite fuel type. You must leverage every fuel source and use them for the appropriate engines. This causes each fuel source to stay abundant and cost effective on the market. There are three fuel groups: alcohol, heating and transportation. Each of the three fuel groups break down into three fuel types. Make sure you cut your gasoline with 10% ethanol and diesel with bio additives. Do not cut kerosene since that's going towards jet fuel. Nuclear fusion is for our warships and thermonuclear warheads. Also, avoid land-based and civilian ship reactors. There were more core meltdowns than the public knew about. Fission is used for boosting.

Materials

Earthworks:

Your masonry needs to capitalize on abundant materials like clay found in sandy uplands. An upland is the land away from any ecosystem's watershed. Flat areas have aquatic plants holding in their banks. Montane areas have rock beds and stepping stones that prevent erosion and purify the water. Study the aquifers of upland areas before mining clay, sand, gravel and rocks so you don't damage the drainage basins.

Metallurgy:

You have construction metals, musical metals, conductive metals, electronic metals, pyrotechnic metals, gases for electric signs or balloons, precious metals for jewelry or currency, and additive metals added to alloys. My alloys use additives with atomic masses and densities similar to the base materials they're added to. The exception to the rule is with the use of carbon since it's the wild card that works with anything. Currency, musical instruments, plaques, statues and time-consuming products like piano plates or engine parts are better off using casting. Everything else will be hot-forged. Use 3D printers on plastics made from silicone, a silicon-based product.

Fuel Alternatives

Alcohol

Ethanol:

Ethanol is mostly produced from sweet corn grown on farms in the prairie states. However, native factories in the cities can use their carbon monoxide waste to make ethanol as well. This reduces emissions from the cities causing all of their petrochemical areas, commonly found in the industrial plazas of cities, to stink less. As mentioned earlier, mix gasoline with 10% ethanol to give it a clearer color with more power, gas mileage and cleaner engines. You'll have more speed and towing capacity. Ethanol is required for F1 cars, dragsters and traditional cigarette lighters.

Methanol:

Methanol is a solid putty used in chaffing dishes at culinary establishments. Most of the time, you'll see these at buffets and catering events inside country clubs. Remember: Don't stock this putty at omelet cooking stations; use butane instead.

Butane:

Even though butane isn't alcohol, it serves alongside methanol at buffets. Like alcohol, it's a light-colored fuel and burns just as cold. Order butane cans for the omelet stations at breakfast areas only (or you'll waste it). For grills, there are three fuel sources and you have to get them right. Run natural gas in restaurant grills, propane for outdoor grilling, and charcoal for portable grills or brewing bourbon.

Heating

Propane:

Use this for welding gear, survival gear, rural heating and heavy cutting torches.

Natural Gas:

For the heating of buildings or restaurant grills. Avoid costly all-electric facilities.

Clean Coal:

Catalytic convertors produce cleaner electricity. In the U.K., use peat instead.

Fuel

Gasoline:

Run gasoline in small trucks or cars used by civilians. All gasoline is unleaded. Use regular gas for cars and trucks rated one-ton or less. Plus is for coupés and mid-level sedans. Native American refineries need to give discounts on plus and avoid producing as much of it since it doesn't sell well. This allows gas stations the ability to offer plus at a cheaper price than the nonnatives. If at any time you have plus laying around past a certain selling period: Market it heavily at the gas station with a discount! Premium/supreme is for high-end coupés like sports cars and luxury sports.

Biodiesel:

Save diesel for freight, shipping, trucking and generators. Biodiesel was discussed earlier in the book. The additives will stretch your supplies and lower the cost of diesel. This is an advantage to natives trying to undercut the nonnatives. Right now, they can only match their prices on fuel and heating. But, once they start infiltrating their businesses with native employees, you can cripple them from the inside. After that, they'll start buying out their businesses and merging them with theirs. This cripples them much faster, funnels resources into their communities and lowers prices. Nuclear-powered warships free up diesel, and thus lowering diesel prices also.

Kerosene:

Kerosene is only for jet fuel. Lighters, even the old-fashioned fancy flip lighters with wicks, should use alcohol instead. It's a much colder, cheaper, abundant and longer-lasting fuel. It won't stink or pollute as much, and won't burn your hand as easily from overheating. Kerosene is refined into three jet fuel types: The first is for military jets, the second tier is for the airlines and the last batch is for executive jets. This HI-LO strategy prevents waste and customers from having to spend more than they should on tickets. Aviation is by far the least fuel-efficient form of travel pound-for-pound.

Traditional Oil:

Oil is for metal-colored paints, lubricants or coolant. When creating paints, study the industry's standards. Watercolors are most commonly used in kids' paintings. Canvas painters will use the oil-based heavy metal versions. If you can make pyrite paint and titanium oxide look just as good as bronze or gold, then you can free up more precious metals for our currency! Be sure to study the metals used in oil-based paints.

Synthetic Oil:

Synthetics are used in the higher end cars or older vehicle makes. Traditional oil will always dominate over synthetics due to cost reasons. There are more trucks, low-end vehicles and people on a tight budget than affluent people or sports car owners.

New Metallurgy

Construction

Silicone Plastics:

Silicone is made from the uplands' sand. Soda companies need glass bottles for better flavor. Crystal requires lead, carbon and boron. Cobalt produces blue hues and bismuth is for purple coloration. Most applications include cologne and perfume bottles. Porcelain pottery requires mother-of-pearl, bismuth and cobalt.

My Alumax Alloy:

Aluminum alloys will replace tin-plated steel cans, steel signs for roads, rebar for construction, portable metal items, sporting goods and all racing materials. Alumax is hot-forged with aluminum, carbon, silicon, beryllium, titanium and magnesium.

My Alkalite Alloy:

Magnesium alloys replace tops on semis, aircraft bodies and boat keels. Use the same metals from Alumax with magnesium, not aluminum, as the primary metal.

Galvanized Steel:

Requires hot-forged iron, manganese, magnesium, vanadium, carbon and zinc. This alloy, unlike other galvanized steel alloys, has zinc mixed inside of the actual metal instead of just running a layer on the outside of the steel. It will not peel off!

Stainless Steel:

All steel placed outdoors needs to be coated with this alloy. Steel starts off with my galvanized base alloy. Then, add 10-26% chromium to create my stainless steel.

My Tetmire Alloy:

Titanium alloys are great for tension wire, powders, colors and medical implants. Use the same metals in Alkalite with titanium instead of magnesium as the base.

My Tungmore Alloy:

Tungsten replaces metals added to tools, weights, jet engines and rocket engines. It's a cast tungsten carbide alloy with tungsten, molybdenum and carbon. Traces of depleted uranium are added if you're manufacturing military ammunition. Add rhenium to the above alloy when you're producing engines for jets and rockets.

Secondary

Nickel-steel:

Coat all steel visible indoors to the public with nickel-steel. This alloy is created by adding 18%+ nickel to my galvanized steel alloy. Nickel shouldn't be wasted in jet engines or automobile rims! Chrome is way better suited for the outdoor stresses than nickel is. Nickel is nicer, but should serve indoor roles only since it's way softer.

Brass Trinity:

There are three types of brass. White brass is the cheapest, and is often used in cable lines and water entry pipes as an alternative to PVC. It deposits minerals and lacks PVC's toxic flavors or chemicals that can leach into your water supply. Yellow brass is seen in horns and the ends of fire hoses. Save red brass for electrical wire.

80/20 Bronze:

Bronze musical instruments require 80/20 cast bronze with small traces of silver, aluminum and nickel. Decorative bronze plaques lack the aluminum and nickel. Tin/zinc solders replace all other solders. Install aluminum, not tin, rain gutters.

Specialty

Depleted Uranium:

Most of the uranium found on Earth is refined into depleted uranium. People use this for the sabot penetrators in artillery shells. Another application is fission-boosted thermonuclear weapons that can shoot down nukes in space. There's no fallout from air blasting! Fallout is created by ground blasting, like in Hiroshima or Nagasaki. Civilian manufacture Vaseline glass for marbles, jacks, glow sticks, rave chucks and crystal products. These items won't increase pollution or make you ill!

Thorium Reactors:

Thorium is reserved for the navy. Make sure your thorium reactors use saltwater for three things: sodium fission boosting, hydrogen and oxygen for boiler pilots, and freshwater for steam turbines and boilers. Use tungsten shields instead of lead, zirconium control rods and air cooling. If there's helium waste, sell it to the public.

Precious Metals:

Oxide-based catalytic convertors and electronics with tantalum, germanium and tellurium will reduce the need for precious metals outside of jewelry or currency. Add pyrite paint to half-titles and monograms with titanium oxide fore-edges on *Holy Bibles*. These two metals work wonders on gourmet candy containers also! Use metal detectors and recycling incentives at landfills to recover more lost metal.

Sustainable Masonry

Materials

Natural Brick:

Natural brick is made from clay found in the uplands for most construction designs. Usage improves the drainage of sandy pine forests and prairie uplands. Check your local uplands' aquifers to make sure they're not deteriorating from mining projects.

Cinderblock:

Cinderblock uses materials found in the uplands also. It forms the backbone of all abode designs. Layer stucco over blocks with wooden beams jutting from rooflines.

Greystone:

Greystone is carved from the upland cliff faces of mountains. It's not impossible to mine mountain ranges without defacing them as long as you space out the mining operations across the region. Use bluestone for the government and 911 buildings.

Brownstone:

Brownstone is a Triassic sandstone used to build villas while greystone is used to build townhouses. Follow similar mining rules listed with greystone and bluestone.

Granite:

Granite is a popular choice for the higher-end countertops in bars or kitchen areas. Unlike quartz, granite requires more maintenance and the necessity for coasters.

Quartz:

Quartz is a popular choice for mid-level countertops. It's highly durable and is much lower maintenance! It lacks the need for coasters and is way easier to wipe clean!

Pea Gravel:

Pea gravel is mandatory for concrete and asphalt mixes used in construction. Just like bull rock listed below, mine the rock from the uplands away from watersheds.

Bull Rock:

Bull rock is utterly crucial for most concrete mixes and water drainage plans.

Review

Power

Drilling Sites:

Stop leaving behind abandoned oil rigs that leak! If there's no oil left in them, then why are they leaking? Invest in smaller handfuls of larger oil rigs that are safer from earthquakes, tidal waves, hurricanes and tornadoes. Run a snake system to make one oil rig do the job of several. Remove excess old oil rigs and recycle their steel for cars.

Cleaner Coal:

Make sure that the clean coal movement uses steam turbines, boilers and dynamos. When following *Saving the United States'* real estate plan, there'll be less land to install underground power making its construction cheaper. Don't add underground power outside the propers; do powerlines instead. Grandfather preexisting nuclear power plants, but do two things: First, encourage them to switch to thorium fusion with tungsten freeing up more lead. Second, encourage them to switch to coal later by guaranteeing scientists who join the navy or National Science Foundation careers.

Green Energy:

Before building a new coal plant, read this checklist first: If you're in space, go solar. If you're a farmer, add a windmill to power your electricity and well. If you have a tourist haven with geothermally-heated water, opt for geothermal. If you have a dam or waterfall nearby, go hydroelectric. Everybody else that's not listed uses coal.

Mining

Reclamation:

Mining companies who are in a financial rut trying to find materials can cut their costs by helping the Department of Roads and Transportation rip decommissioned roads out. They can do this after implementing Chapter Three from my first book. They can either recycle the material, sell it to companies raw or make products for people.

CHAPTER EIGHT

Digital Electronics

Overview

Digital

Liberation:

Chapter Eight unveils your cities' future media formats. This is the urban quadrant geared for the second-generation urban natives and the third-generation rural ones.

The USBs:

All electronics manufactured by natives are digital devices utilizing USB flash drives with MP4 files. They'll replace DVDs, Blue Ray, MP3 handhelds, CDs, tape cassette and vinyl record turntables for good. They're going to be used by many generations!

The Buttons:

The devices feature buttons similar to the ones found on twentieth-century devices. This grants older generations the ability to have a simpler device to learn how to master and makes them gladly chose these newer devices over their older ones. This also allows the younger, more tech-savvy generations demanding the most from their devices to have what they desire. These digital devices forever replace analog.

Distribution:

These devices can be sold at music, movie, game and electronics stores worldwide. They use small, handheld jewel cases reminiscent to CDs. You slide them open with your thumb to reveal a small 2x4 booklet with the USB next to it. Game stores can sell old-fashioned 1990's-style game cartridges and cases featuring metallic "USB" teeth instead of the plastic teeth seen from yesteryears. They're quite durable too!

Computers

Hard and Solid:

While most competitors are making larger hard disk drives (aka HDDs), we're making smaller solid-state drives (aka SSDs) more affordable! Pretty soon, the mainframes within government supercomputers will be the only things left using hard drives!

Media Formats

Cameras

Photography:

Professional cameras will have a power button, shutter slide, red-eye option and zoom scrolls for ease of use. This makes them idiot proof! Professional photographers can tack on other components to their cameras. Cameras come standard with a USB port. Generic cameras have been rendered obsolete due to modern-day cell phones.

Camcorders:

Video cameras come in three basic flavors: First, the GoPro. Second, the professional video camera. The new professional camera will replace the larger older ones with add-ons. Last, is the digital surveillance camera with links and USB ports for records.

Cinema:

Digital film can help movie theatres play the best content for modern-day 3D action films. Televisions no longer depend upon traditional cable or satellite service providers, but instead, fiber internet connections. Replace all telecommunications poles with underground optical "fiber" lines, unless you're crossing a body of water.

Recordings

Jukeboxes:

Digital jukeboxes are for bars. They can change "records" that double as cooling fans.

Turntables:

Digital turntables replace vinyl ones and can be placed in decorative award plaques.

Recorders:

Digital recorders are used by researchers for logs and musicians to create "demos".

Stereos:

Digital stereos still get AM/FM. Businesses have their own internet radio station.

Boomboxes:

Smaller, digital boomboxes allow for break dancing, parties and light concerts.

Communications

Business:

Business phones come in two versions: First, the corded desktop VoIP (voice over internet protocol) phone. They feature options like flash, call waiting and extension numbers. Second, the cordless WIFI handset. Originally geared for home phone use, these handsets are great for areas away from offices. For example, an ICU patient's nurse could have one of these phones while the reception area has desktop phones.

Mobiles:

Cellular phones consolidated the roles of home phone, mobile phone, pay phone, disposable film, calculator and PDA. Most people opt out of buying camcorders, flash lights, wrist watches, stop watches and alarm clocks by just using their smartphones.

Pagers:

Digital pagers are used by emergency services, maintenance staffs and restaurants informing their customers when their tables are ready. Pagers aren't useless or obsolete; they just need to become digitalized! Analog pagers have become obsolete.

Radios:

Satellite Radio:

Unlike military personnel deployed overseas, civilians have access to an extensive electronics grid. Therefore, digital radio stations render AM/FM obsolete to civilians.

Military Radio:

Personnel deployed overseas in rural parts of the World don't have access to an expensive electronics grid like our civilians back at home do. Bases need FM because they have the most radio operators, which can cause interference. Camps field AM due to its superior range. Rescue teams deploy CW (aka HAM) radios and crash pilots send signals via mirrors. Frogmen (divers) get extremely-low frequency radios.

Light Radio:

The U.S. Navy requires blue lasers on their submarines to facilitate rapid underwater communications. A sub sends a signal behind them to another allied vessel. Then, the signal is slowed down and converted into sound. After that, a Morse code operator translates the message to the watercraft's crew. U.S. naval bases need to install covert underwater listening posts so they can communicate with submerged subs.

Computers

Office PC: $1,200 USD

The office PC is used by lower-level employees in white-collar office buildings. They have large flat-screen monitors, corded keyboards and mouse setups, external speakers, subwoofers and printers/copiers. Instead of hard drives, use one-terabyte solid-state drives, 32 gigabytes of RAM and the fastest processors. They feature a simpler LINUX-style operating system so they can run older programs like MSDOS, MSRUN and AutoCAD. Companies using them will have their own intranet LAN lines.

Business Laptop: $500 USD

Business laptops are given to office managers who have to take work home with them. Instead of hard drives, use 500-gigabyte solid-state drives, 16 gigabytes of RAM and fairly fast processors. Smaller screens, batteries and speakers plus a lack of a mouse reduces costs. Unlike office PCs, business laptops have cordless Wi-Fi internet.

Personal Laptop: $250 USD

Personal laptops are for students, avid gamers and home usage. They feature larger screens, better speakers, a cordless mouse and 8 gigabytes of RAM to satisfy the modern gamer on a budget. These laptops have 250-gigabyte solid-state drives and smaller processors. Both laptops have similar operating systems and cordless Wi-Fi.

Business Tablet: $100 USD

Business tablets are for executives and businesses reducing customer paperwork. They feature their businesses' custom POS systems and 50-gigabyte drives. Employee paperwork, like employee manuals or inventory/record books, should stay printed.

Personal Tablet: $50 USD

Personal tablets have 5-gigabyte drives supporting disability readers' audiobooks and color pictures. "On-the-go" handbooks are best suited as e-books for smartphones.

Consoles: $300 USD

Video game consoles have free Wi-Fi, 500-gigabyte solid-state drives, insurance options, "Indy" support, arcade downloads and data transfer from obsolete consoles.

Handhelds: $150 USD

Handheld video game devices use smaller USB cartridges, 50-gigabyte drives and similar perks found on consoles. They'll look like the Nintendo DSs or Sony PSPs!

Review

Entertainment

The Gaming Industry:

Modern 64-bit games are great for quests, military games and horror. The 32-bit games are great for sports, racing games and girls. Vintage 16-bit games are great for boy's arcade-style action games. Classic 8-bit games are great for collectors and little kid's adventures. Supporting independent game makers bolsters the amount of game titles for you. Remember, you don't need more bits to have more speed and graphics, just more RAM or hard drive. Also, increasing megahertz is important. Upgrade packages on consoles allow them to sell for up to 15 years instead of every five years.

The Movie Studios:

Never release more than a trilogy. (Ex: *Godfather*, *Lethal Weapon*, *Death Wish* and *Indiana Jones*.) Some movies only have enough content for one good sequel. (Ex: *Terminator*, *Alien/Aliens*) Some movies were designed to stand alone. (Ex: *Ninja Turtles* and *Scarface*) There are only two outcomes: They want more of it or hate it.

The Musicians:

The rule of thumb is to obey three key rules. First, limit singles (the album type, not the radio songs) to demos. Second, limit extended plays (aka EPs) to "B-sides". B-sides are the records containing leftover material that didn't make the cut for studio albums. If you're going to make an album, make it a true label production (aka LP).

Phones

Smart-flips:

The best strategy for cell phones is to offer three types of folding smartphones. One, is $1,500 and has a seven-inch screen. The next is $1,000 with a six-inch screen. The third is a $750 compact phone with a five-inch screen. Connect two glass screens to a rotating glass rod. Also, larger rims prevent you from accidentally closing videos.

CHAPTER NINE

Musical Equipment

Overview

Strategy

Manufacturing:

This chapter teaches natives how to build superior instruments with better prices, how to select instruments properly and how to tune them correctly. The timber plots from the country's forested park systems are required in order to give you a price and material edge over the nonnatives. Some of the species listed are endangered.

Bands

Band Equipment:

Drum sets, electric basses, electric guitars, acoustic basses and acoustic guitars are all covered in this chapter. I used drier timbers with nice names, color and grain for guitars. Drums use sweet timbers with boring names, color and grain. From heaviest to lightest, this is the order: head/fretboard > binding > frame > body > neck. Guitar fretboards need to have the smoothest, oiliest, hardest and tightest-grained woods.

The Orchestras:

Orchestral arrangements and their instruments' designs are also covered. Bass string instruments obey the opposite rules: Lighter woods are used in their interiors and heavier woods are used for their bodies. They need a light, flexible top to carry sound vibrations out. Lighter hardwoods shall replace conifer wood for good. Flutes are woodwinds, so stop using silver. It raises the pitch so much that you have to make retarded-looking candy cane flutes. Just stick with the fifes, piccolos, treble flutes and concert flutes made out of ironwood. Chrome is better than silver when making keys.

Piano Designs:

Pianos are given lighter designs and new materials are selected for their hammers, soundboards and strings. A $1,200 to $16,000 piano surpasses a $400,000+ piano in sound quality. (FY2019 USD) The lighter designs can be rolled around one-handed.

Drumming Designs

Drum Shells

Drum Kit Designs:

Bearing edges are baseball bats on kicks, 30s on floors, 45s on rack toms and 60s on snares. Resonant edges are sharper while batter edges are round-overs. For reinforcement hoops, use blue ash on entries, green ash on mid-levels and white ash on pro kits. Give heavier triple-flanged hoops to toms, heavy triple-flanges on wooden snares and heavy die-casts on metal snares. Add five to six lugs on rack toms, six to eight lugs on floor toms and eight to ten lugs on snares/kicks. Issue aluminum hardware with chrome-plated entries, satin chrome mid-levels and satin nickel pros.

Drum Shells: *Plywood*

Entry-level shells are vertical-ply drums, mid-level shells are horizontal-ply drums and professional-level shells are glue-free variants of horizontal plies. Try 9-ply rack toms, 8-ply floor toms and 7-ply kick drums to blend pitches. Reinforcement hoops are 9-plys. For custom boutique sets, do 10-plys on cherry kits and 11-plys on poplar kits.

Snare Drums: *Blocks*

Entry-level snare drums are 14-piece vertical staves, mid-level snares are 42-piece horizontal segments and the professional snares are horizontal bentwood drums. Piccolo snare drums use horizontal hollow tree trunks as "solid shells". Custom shop snares and firecracker-style marching snares apply cold-rolling on entry-levels, dry-hammering on mid-levels and casting on pro-levels. Add evershine and natural finish.

Drum Setups

Choices of Woods:

Bright kits use sweet birch shells with sugar maple snares. Warm kits use yellow birch shells with field maple snares. Dark kits have silver birch shells with black maple snares. The other woods that aren't listed are for building guitars and orchestra instruments.

Choices of Heads:

Frosted in orchestra, Kevlar for marching, ebony on bass resonant heads, coated for snare batters or vintage sounds, FiberSkyns on hand percussion, self-muted for mid-levels, oil-filled towards entry-levels and clears on everything else that's not listed.

Drum Sizes

Orchestra Drums:

My timpani sizes are 8", 10", 12" and 14" for the first line. The second line is 16", 18", 20" and 22". The third line is 24", 26", 28" and 30". The last line is 32", 34", 36" and 38". Always build cast copper shells. Pair thick, frosted, etched heads with way lower tunings. Stop using snares and bass drums! Gong drums are for tribal political parties. Do 80" at leagues, 70" at nations, 60" for tribes, 50" for bands and 40" for our clans.

Marching Drums:

Marching bands need a 36" x 14" drum with a 3-ply shell on a rotating wagon at the rear. Wagon basses are 34" x 14", 32" x 14", 30" x 14" and 28" x 14" with 4-plys. Bass drums are 26" x 14", 24" x 14", 22" x 14" and 20" x 14" with 5-plys. Field drums are 17" x 14", 16" x 14", 15" x 14" and 14" x 14" with 6-plys, fat snare baskets and 7-mil resonant heads. Piccolo snares are 15" x 4.5", 14" x 4.5", 13" x 4.5" and 12" x 4.5" with solid shells (hollowed trunk), standard baskets and 3-mil resonant heads. Copper firecrackers are 14" x 8", 12" x 8", 10" x 8" and 8" x 8" with small snare baskets and 5-mil resonant heads. Add sparkle-finished PVC wraps with natural oil interior plies.

Personalized Sets:

Drum sets get 20" x 17" kick drums, 16" x 16" and 14" x 14" floor toms ("tunnels" are legless), 12" x 8" and 10" x 7" rack toms. Add 13" x 6" ballad snares with small snare baskets and 2-mil resonant heads. Offer matte finishes both inside and out on shells. Put rubber spacers on tom mounts and use virgin kicks. Obsolete kicks include 26", 24" and 22" sizes. For floors/tunnels, 20" and 18" toms are unnecessary. With rack toms, 14" and 13" dimensions are too. As for ballad snares, 15" and 14" sizes are also.

Cymbals

Cymbal Designs:

Always use cast 80/20 bronze (aka B20), computer hammering, heavy pin lathing and evershine. Inspect consistency on hand-hammered cymbals and pliability. For sheet bronze cymbals, do B20 on pros, B12 for mid-levels and B8 for entry-level box sets.

Cymbal Sizes:

Rides/Swishes: 24", 22" and 20" mediums. Crash Rides: 23", 21" and 19" medium-thins. Pangs: 21", 20" and 19" medium-thins. Crashes: 20", 19", 18", 17" and 16" extra-thins. Chinas: 18", 17" and 16" thins. Hi-hats: 15", 14" and 13" with medium-thin tops and medium bottoms. Splashes: 12", 10" and 8" extra-thins. Ice Bells: 10", 8" and 6" heavies for stacking. Clashes: 20" and 18" sets of German (medium-heavy), Viennese (medium) and French (medium-thin). *Finger Cymbals are extra-heavy.

Guitar Designs

Guitars

Guitar Models:

Fretboards are cocobolo rosewood on entry-levels, Pau Ferro ironwood on mid-levels and ebony on professional-level parlors. For strings and pickups, always pick steel. Entry-levels get heavy strings, mid-levels the standard sizes and professionals need lighter strings. Oil the interiors, stain the acoustics and stain/lacquer electric guitars.

Electric Models:

Electric guitars get solid bodies, semi-hollow bodies and hollow bodies as their entry-level, mid-level and pro-level designs. For the knobs and pickups, plate their entry-levels with chrome, mid-levels with satin chrome and the pro tiers with stain nickel.

Electric Guitars:

Guitars need purpleheart frames, jarrah bodies, bloodwood bindings and redheart necks. For fretboard dots, use the shells of shellfish on entry-levels, mother-of-pearl on mid-levels and pearl on pro-levels. Electric basses should always pair wenge as frames, zebrawood for bodies, bubinga on bindings and black korina in their necks.

Acoustics

Acoustic Guitars:

Acoustic parlors and basses always follow this formula: For frames, entry-levels get black oak, mid-levels do red oak and professional-levels have white oak. For bodies, entry-levels get magnolia, mid-levels have sweet cherry and professional-levels need claro black walnut. For bindings, entry-levels use myrtle, mid-levels get dogwood and pros use laurel. For necks, use farm-raised Peruvian mahogany on entries, Honduran mahogany on mid-levels and Cuban mahogany on all of the professional-level guitars.

Acoustic Finishes:

For nuts and saddles, use ox bone on the entry-levels, bison bone on the mid-levels and buffalo bone on the pros. Neck dots will use farm-raised culled ivory. Put black rhino on entries, white rhino on mid-levels and elephant on pros. Make sure you have timber barrens who'll invest in park systems around the world. This allows them to farm-raise all of their required bone, ivory and endangered tropical hardwoods.

Orchestra Designs

Orchestras

String Instruments:

Violins, violas, cellos and double basses use these designs: Use red alder blocks and linings, basswood bass bars and sound posts, Khaya bodies and scrolls, and black willow tops. Use snakewood chinrests with Brazilwood boxes, tailpieces, buttons and pegs. Use beech bridges, ebony fingerboards, catgut strings and finally, snakewood horsehair bows. The interior woods get oil and dark-stained exterior woods get gloss lacquers. Use segmented entries, semi-hollow body for mid-levels and hollow body for pro-levels. Use farm-raised African blackwood for woodwind instruments with natural oil inside and out. Woodwinds have chrome hardware. Stock a black gloss $16,000 FY2019 USD concert grand piano for guest pianists. Make everything lighter!

Drum Division

The Percussion Line:

There are four percussion tables and they require colorful yarn mallets. Farm-raising endangered species in park systems' rainforests lowers timber costs. Use padauk in place of rosewood plates. It's superior in quality and way cheaper! Casting yellow brass musical plates and pipes can lower the cost of labor, thus reducing the instrument's price. This prevents percussion prices from topping $2,000 FY2019 USD.

The Copper Section:

Copper sections will have four lines with four players per line. Each player has one drum with lyre pedals. Use even numbers for timpani diameters to create better pitch differences between drums. Diameters favor even numbers or numbers divisible by five. Only snare drums and drum shell depths break these rules. Bullets obey these principles too. Using casting and chrome keys keeps costs under $2,000 FY2019 USD.

The Bronze Division:

Cymbal divisions will have one gong and one clash section. Always use cast 80/20 bronze for superior sound and to reduce labor cost. Use extra-heavy gongs. An 18" and 19" cymbal will have the same pitch difference as a 10" and 12" drum does. Giant gongs are at temples in Asia and giant gong drums will be at tribes' headquarters.

Orchestra Sections

Symphonic

String Division: 32

Harp Section: 4 x 4 = 16

Use lap harps, arch harps, lever harps and pedal harps made from hardwood timber.

Bass Section: 4 x 4 = 16

Use the violins, violas, cellos and double basses (upright basses) listed in this chapter.

Piper Division: 32

Woodwind Section: 4 x 4 = 16

Use flutes, clarinets, oboes and bassoons made out of farm-raised black ironwood.

Brass Section: 4 x 4 = 16

Use trumpets, trombones, saxophones and saxhorns made out of cast yellow brass.

Cymbal Division: 32

Clash Section: 4 x 4 = 16

Use taal, French, Vienna and German style clashes made out of cast 80/20 bronze.

Gong Section: 4 x 4 = 16

Use tam-tam, wind, Chau and symphonic gongs made out of cast 80/20 bronze.

Drum Division: 32

Drum Section: 4 x 4 = 16

Use four copper timpani sets split between 16 drummers using large mallets.

Percussion Section: 4 x 4 = 16

Use glockenspiels, xylophones, vibraphones and padauk wood marimbas.

Console Keyboards: 4

Use one ottavino, archicembalo, celesta, piano, grand piano and conductor.

Ensemble Size: *50-120 people*

Marching

Pipe Division: 32

Woodwind Section: 4 x 4 = 16

Use flutes, clarinets, oboes and bassoons made out of farm-raised African blackwood.

Brass Section: 4 x 4 = 16

Use trumpets, trombones, saxophones and saxhorns made out of cast yellow brass.

Drum Line: 16

Drum Section: 4 x 4 = 16

Use side drums, field drums, piccolo snares and copper "firecracker" snare drums.

Wagon Drum: 1

The wagon drum will be spun around and struck behind the marching procession.

Conductor: 1

The conductor will carry a baton at the front that they twirl around for the crowds.

Ensemble Size: *20-50 people*

Church

Choir: 36

Small choirs are usually 12, standard choirs are 24 and large choirs 36 people.

Organ: 1

Pipe organs are for large assemblies and concert organs are for smaller ones.

Ensemble Size: *8-20 people*

Notes

*Contemporary service bands, like most bands, are roughly three to eight people.

*There are four divisions x four sections per division x four versions of an instrument.

*Use fifes, piccolos, treble flutes and concert flutes; no candy cane-shaped flutes!

Piano Construction

Methods

New Materials:

Cross-laminated white meranti is for the ultra-thin pin blocks, rims and back posts. Tulip poplar gives you better soundboards and piano keys. Poplar is stronger than Sitka spruce. Add ultra-thin hornbeam bridges, pin blocks and actions. It's stronger than beech! Build a thinner cast magnesium alloy plate with a cast yellow brass veneer. Construct the strings out of my galvanized steel alloy. Put copper winding over bass strings and phosphorus bronze over the treble strings. Install hophornbeam hammers. It's stronger and prettier than hornbeam! Toss in farm-raised and culled ivory to build black sharps/flats and white natural keys. Finish with yellow brass lyres.

New Purchases:

For consoles, entry-levels are for aspiring students, mid-levels are for hobbyists and professionals are for the true gigging pianist. The upright pianos are procured by organizations that allow pianists to play them. They don't have to be moved and their guest pianists don't have to buy them either. Baby grands are for stately homes or collectors, parlor grands are for fine-dining restaurants or country clubs, ballroom grands are for cruise ships and hotels, and concert grands are for theatric halls used by symphonic orchestras. Great houses may have baby grand pianos worth millions in decorative upgrades! The prices listed below will be displayed in FY2019 USDs.

Prices

Console Pianos:

Entry Consoles: $120 to $300 *(Beginner Players – Children)*

Mid Consoles: $300 to $600 *(Intermediate Players – Teens)*

Pro Consoles: $600 to $1,200 *(Advanced Players – Adults)*

Grand Pianos:

Baby Grands: $1,200 to $2,000 *(Upper Class – Collectors)*

Parlor Grands: $2,000 to $4,000 *(Hospitality Organizations)*

Ballroom Grands: $4,000 to $8,000 *(Travel Organizations)*

Concert Grands: $8,000 to $16,000 *(Orchestra Groups)*

Review

Production

Folk Orchestras:

Countries should study my plans for both of the orchestra types. They can use their countries' regional instruments as alternatives to the listed instruments. They should still use my line, section and division rules. This allows what might be considered a rare instrument very few people play to become more abundant than ever in their culture. Also, it preserves their traditional music and folk music for many generations.

Appropriate Pricing:

Prices for your entry-level instruments need to be no more than $120 to $300 USD. Prices for the mid-level instruments need to be around $300 to $600 USD. Prices for professional instruments should be between $600 to $1,200 USD. Custom shop metal snare drums are $400 to $800 USD. Concert organs will obey similar piano pricing rules while custom pipe organs in churches can be as costly as you want them to be.

Drummers

Drum Evolution:

Tabors came before the firecracker, which preceded rack toms. Tarols inspired the piccolo's development, which led to ballad snares. The long drum predates the field drum, which came before the floor/tunnel tom. Gong drums predate the side drum, which inspired kick drums. Drum sets have two pairs; each pair has a higher-pitched tube and low-pitched shallow one. Therefore, keep snare pitches lower than toms.

Drum Balancing:

With proper timpani lines, there's no need for their snare drums, bass drums or gong drums. With proper soprano firecrackers, alto piccolos, tenor field drums, baritone side drums, contrabaritone wagon drums and ceremonial subcontrabaritone bass drums: There's no need for marching timpani drums. You had it totally backwards!

CHAPTER TEN

Publishing Books

Overview

Printing

Proper Books:

Chapter Ten focuses on the art of writing books. The word counts, page counts, page sizes, paper thicknesses, paper colors, ink colors, ink grades, book covers, font types, font sizes and font stylization patterns inside of the books are covered in this chapter.

Schooling

The Curriculum:

The natives will follow my new education system based on reading books. It's way better than focusing on intensive testing or homework! Chemistry classes will teach the periodic table by using math last. They start with the families of construction metals, additive metals, coloring metals and pyrotechnic metals first. This helps the children understand why those elements are so important. They should have daily science labs with test tubes and beakers. Science classes always have yearly in-class projects and annual field trips. Privately owned nurseries are rated as 1As. Private schools and small institutes are often 2As. Daycare hold naps, preschool playgroup has toys, pre-k has arts and crafts, and kindergartens have story times and "blabs".

Books

Lesson Planning:

Schedule daily lesson plans, weekly in-class assignments, bi-monthly homework, monthly typed book reports, bi-quarterly quizzes, quarterly tests and semi-annual state scantron exams. Each class's teacher will wheel in a cart full of books for a bi-weekly read. Libraries will have hundreds of copies of each title and hundreds of titles. This is better than having a few copies of thousands of titles. The last thirty minutes of class is set aside for in-class book reading. Math classes hold tutoring.

Book Classifications

Fiction

Novelette:

Novelettes are for primary school students' monthly reviews. Use 30-60 pages. Offer 3x6 sizes, premium matte hardbacks and dust jackets, 70lb scented cream paper, black and white interiors, and 9-point Constantia/san-serif fonts. Use 8-16 chapters. *Some genres include girls' poetry and boys' almanac titles for elementary schools.*

Novella:

Novellas are used for middle school students' monthly abstracts. Use 60-120 pages. Offer 4x7 sizes, premium matte hardbacks without dust jackets, 70lb scented cream paper, black and white interiors, and 10-point Constantia/san-serif fonts. Use 8-16 chapters. *Some genres include women's comedies and adventures for young boys.*

Novel:

Novels are for high school students' monthly book reports. Use 120-250 pages. Offer 5x8 sizes, premium matte paperbacks with optional raised text, 70lb scented cream paper, black and white interiors and 11-point Constantia/san-serif fonts. Use 8-16 chapters. *Some genres include boys' mystery and girls' romance for middle schools.*

Epic:

Epics are used for college admissions' articles. Use 250-500 pages. Offer 6x9 sizes, standard matte oak hardcovers, 50lb scented cream paper, black and white interiors, and 12-point Constantia/san-serif fonts. Use 16-32 booklets split between two collection modules. Use yellow brass page tips, yellow brass key locks and lettrines. *Genres include sagas, thrillers and sci-fi. High schoolers send reports to admissions.*

Anthology:

Anthologies are for nursery school teachers. Use 500-1,200 pages. Offer 8x10 sizes, standard matte oak hardcovers, 50lb scented cream paper, standard color gloss page inserts and 14-point Constantia/san-serif fonts. Use 16-32 small books split via two collection modules. Use two-page popups, yellow brass page tips, yellow brass key locks and lettrines. *Some genres include poetry and kindergarteners' short stories.*

Follow novelette rules on flash poetry booklets. There are four types of flash below 1,000 words. Short story books are for toddlers. Use gloss hardbacks, 70lb white paper, standard color interiors, landscape orientations and two-page popups.

Education

Journal (Book):

Academic journals are used for primary school students' monthly reports. Use 30-60 pages. Offer 3x6 sizes, gloss hardbacks and dust jackets, 70lb white paper, premium color gloss insert pages and 8-point Cambria/Calibri fonts. Use 8-16 chapters in total.

Monograph:

Monographs are for middle school students' monthly reports. Use 60-120 pages. Offer 4x7 sizes, gloss hardbacks, 70lb white paper, premium color gloss insert pages and 9-point Cambria/Calibri fonts. Use 8-16 chapters. *They never have two authors.*

Treatise:

Treatises are for high school students' monthly reports. Use 120-250 pages. Offer 5x8 sizes, gloss paperbacks, 70lb white paper, premium color gloss insert pages and 10-point Cambria/Calibri fonts. Use 8-16 chapters. *Some genres include biographies.*

Compendium:

Compendiums are for math/language textbooks. Use 250-500 pages. Offer 6x9 sizes, gloss metal hardcovers, 50lb white paper, standard color gloss insert pages and 11-point Cambria/Calibri fonts. Use 16-32 booklets split by two units. *Use keyhole locks.*

Omnibus:

Omnibuses are for science/history textbooks. Use 500-1,200 pages. Offer 8x10 sizes, gloss metal hardcovers, 50lb white paper, standard color gloss insert pages and 12-point Cambria/Calibri fonts. Use 16-32 books split into two units. *Use keyhole locks.*

Chapters

Fiction Sizes: 2-4 pages is small, 4-8 pages is medium, 8-16 pages is maximum.

Education Sizes: 4-6 pages is small, 6-10 pages is medium, 10-18 pages is large.

Paragraphs: Fiction tabs paragraphs, nonfiction spaces them. Use 1x spacing.

Paragraph Sizes: 2-4 lines is small, 5-7 is medium, 8-10 is the maximum size.

Line Spacing: Multiple on protectors, double on titles, single on subsections.

Body Spacing: Single on paragraphs, 0.8x on verse/stanza bullets and lines.

Bullet Lists: Use 5-7 section pages. Bullet subsections, verses and stanzas.

Fiction Breaks: First page's top 1/3rd blank, last page's bottom 1/3rd blank.

Education Breaks: 1st page is title page, 2nd is overview, last is the review.

Reference Books

Handbook:

Handbooks are for science classes' weekly assignments. Use 60-120 pages. Offer 3x6 sizes, bonded leather hardcovers and cloth dust jackets, 30lb scritta paper, standard color gloss insert pages and 7-point Cambria/Calibri fonts. The 4x7s are for middle schools and 5x8s for high schools. *Pls' handbooks use 6x9 sizes, gloss paperbacks, 50lb white paper, black and white interiors, and 10-point Cambria/Calibri font types.*

Chrestomathy:

Chrestomathies are used by high school language classes. Use 120-250 pages. Offer 4x7 sizes, bonded leather hardcovers, 30lb scritta paper, black and white interiors, and 8-point Cambria/Calibri fonts. Use A-Z keyhole tabs. *These books help you translate words from one language into another. (Ex: Spanish-to-English dictionaries)*

Dictionary:

Dictionaries are used by primary school language classes. Use 250-500 pages. Offer 5x8 sizes, bonded leather softcovers, 30lb scritta paper, black and white interiors, and 9-point Cambria/Calibri fonts. Add A-Z keyhole tabs in. *List definitions and uses.*

Thesaurus:

Thesauri are used by middle school language classes. Use 500-1,000 pages. Offer 6x9 sizes, leather hide hardcovers, 20lb scritta paper, black and white interiors and 10-point Cambria/Calibri fonts. Use dual A-Z keyhole tabs and one "division" divider flip tab. The two division modules split synonyms and antonyms. *Use rope ties as locks.*

Encyclopedia:

Encyclopedias are for history classes' weekly assignments. Use 1,000-2,400 pages. Offer 8x10 sizes, leather hide hardcovers, 20lb scritta paper, standard color gloss page inserts and 11-point Cambria/Calibri fonts. Use two testament module flip tabs to separate the four division modules. Give flip-tabs to the division modules too. Use 32-64 keyhole tabs and rope ties as locks. The covers together in the shelf display an image across their spines. *You can annul an encyclopedia's bible editions every year.*

Bookmarks: Use gloss for education, matte for fiction and felt ribbons for reference.

Testaments: Encyclopedias and law books are the only categories using testaments.

Protectors: Protector pages require thicker, rougher and more colorful paper.

Constructing Books

The Holy Bible

The Holy Books. Use 1,000-2,400 pages. Offer 8x10 sizes, leather treasure covers with the reader's initials in titanium oxide, 20lb scritta paper with fore-edges dipped in titanium oxide, standard color gloss insert pages and 11-point Cambria/Calibri fonts. There are 64 core books, two bonus books and two testaments. For the two annexed books, *Song of Songs* is Old Testament and *Revelation* is New Testament. This gives you 32-64 books + two bonus books. Give them matching-colored cover backing, protector pages and felt bookmark ribbon. Place reviews on the blank barcode page next to the monogram page. Signatures and initials are in blue if the paper is white.

The Front Matter:

Half-titles are oil-based pyrite-painted titles on the front of the first protector. This is for autographs signed in black pen. If it's white paper, use blue pens. The rear side of the page has a color frontispiece picture. Make sure the protectors are thick, color-coordinated, heavy paper. Its first scritta page is the first true page with a full-title. Pages four through five are the introduction. Page four has an epigraph (witty quote describing the book) with a dedication below. Below the dedication is a picture. Page five has the foreword signed by another person above the preface signed by the author. One supports the author and the other describes the book. Pages six through seven are the table of contents. Do not list anything after the contributions section.

The Main Body:

Pages eight through nine are the two standard color glossed insert pages of the Old Testament listing books and pictures. Page ten is the synopsis. Page eleven is *Genesis'* title page. Treat books like chapter title pages; their second page is their overviews and their last page on the left their reviews. Number chapters/sections. Start on the right and end on the left. If you can't, add study guide stuff in and avoid blank filler pages. The last page on the right is a summary before the two-page New Testament. After that, the page on the left is the synopsis and the other, *Matthew's* title page. The last page on the right is the summary followed closely by a two-page conclusion.

The Conclusion:

The conclusion's left-hand page has the afterword with typed initials at the top-right listing thanks by a supporting voice. The postface is below that with typed initials by the author. On the right-hand page, the acknowledgments are located at the top, the "epitome" quote describing the book is dead-center and a picture is beneath that.

Modules:

Fiction Rules:

In fiction, use a prologue page on the left after the contents and place the first page of chapter one on the right. The last page of the final chapter dies on the left with its epilogue on the right. (One left page is the beginning and the other the ending.) Epics and anthologies get a two-page collection module after the two-page contents and before the prologue/start. An intermission page is on the right, after the last page of the first module's final chapter. After that, the next two-page collection module will be visible. Then, the next page, seen on the left, is the "intercourse". Their second modules' first chapter title page begins on the right. The last chapter ends on the left with its epilogue page on the right. *Fiction and nonfiction education lack divisions.*

Nonfiction Rules:

In nonfiction, use a synopsis page on the left and a chapter title page on the right. Top-down on the title page, list: the chapter number, chapter name, picture and sections directory. The next page is an overview and the last page on the left is a review. On the right, there's the next chapter's title page. Repeat this until the last chapter dies on the left revealing a summary page on the right. My directions on building the Holy Bible will show you how to make nonfiction books. Only bibles in nonfiction reference use divisions inside testaments; they obey similar module rules.

Back Matter:

First, is the two-page conclusion listed on the table of contents. Next, is the optional appendix. The left page has the title, "annex directory" subtitle, picture and directory for navigating the appendix. At the end, place a reference page on the right. Then, there's the seven-page contributions section. The left page is an index for the back matter. On the right, place the about the author in and a picture of the author at the bottom-right corner. Don't sign this page! The next two pages are the glossary. You can add a bibliography with an even number of pages or post one online if necessary. And finally, you have the colophon on the left. That's the last scritta page in the book.

Rear Protector:

While the last scritta page lists the contributors above the legal and citing listings, the right side has a standard color endpiece mural on the backside of the protector page. The other side has an oil-based pyrite painted monogram, or logo. It lists the author or group of authors. Below that area is where you pin all of the ribbon sticker awards.

Reminders:

Paperbacks lack protectors, so the first and last pair of pages are interior ones. Use an even page count not divisible by four to get two blank pages. Postscript a letter on the front and salutation on the back. Below, sign your initials. Use blue pen if paper is white. (Addendums include editors' erratum/authors' corrigendum corrections.)

Review

Titles

Revisions:

Align gutters to the left in print preview. Create new editions of historic book titles you wish to keep in your libraries. Remove excess matter pages and correct the books with my setup rules. Adjust their font styles, sizes, line spacings and supporting chapter pages as needed. This gives you a word count equal to or less than the ranges listed below on this page. Break down English dictionaries and thesauri into old, middle and high language development periods so they can fit into my word counts.

Interiors:

Use 0.5" margins with 0.25" gutters. Some books, especially 6x9s and 8x10s, get 0.5" gutters. I use 1.5x spacing on matter pages with font sizes equal to or two sizes bigger than the body, 1.25x spacing on supporting body pages, 1.2x spacing on fiction bodies and single-spaced bodies on nonfiction books. Paragraph bullets require 0.8x spacing.

Word Counts:

Listed below are the historic word counts for all book sizes. Books swelled up in word count once they printed thinner paper and book covers. The thinner paper was only supposed to have been used to make larger books thinner and easier to carry. Anthologies have no rules and can adjust font sizes or line spacing to fit their needs. The Library of Congress shall serve as our national book archive for all English titles.

Word Counts

Short Story: Under 4,000

Novelette: 4,000 to 10,000

Novella: 10,000 to 24,000

Novel: 24,000 to 60,000

Epic: 60,000 to 150,000

Box Sets

Anthologies: Poetry/Story Collection

Completed Works: Works of Author

Collected Works: Entire Book Series

Selected Works: Book Subseries

Tetralogies: Four-Book Series

CHAPTER ELEVEN

The Printing Industry

Overview

Offsets

The Gazettes:

Newsprint companies should replace their newspapers with almanacs, crossword puzzles, connect-the-dots and coloring books. Presses could use standardized book sizes doing away with the current tabloid, Berliner and broadsheet sizes. They'll need higher quality newsprint paper that's thicker and whiter in color. They can offset the cost increases by reducing the page counts and page sizes. Taped spines prevent their productions from becoming a loose mess and are much safer than staples; staples could fly around in the press rooms. Paper boys could supply your local businesses.

The Directories:

The idea of phone books for homes is obsolete just like newspapers due to the advent of smartphones and the Internet. Phone books resting next to business landlines at organizations aren't. Be sure to ditch the white and grey pages. Use yellow pages for business listings, green pages for non-profit listings and blue pages for governmental and emergency services like local hospitals, veterinarians or clinics. All home phones should be automatically enrolled in the no-call list without even having to ask for it.

Coated

The Magazines:

Magazines are way too big! If you use smaller page sizes, then the cost of shipping and handling goes down considerably. Now, you can afford to reduce the number of ads you have. With less ads, you'll require even less pages. With less pages, costs go down again. Once costs go down again, you'll have enough money left over to use thicker paper with glued spines. With thicker paper and glued spines, 24-48-page magazines will look as fat as 120-page magazines do. Focus on educational nonfiction topics sold to organizations' lounges. Digests are for little kids; comics are for teens and popular sizes are for adults. Obey this rule: E-printing is digital – the rest aren't.

Scholarly Lounges

Organizations

Broadsides:

Bullface: Neighborhood blocks often nail up a bullface listing lost items or animals.

Poster: Posters are used to advertise venues. They're used in kids' bedrooms too!

Billboard: Each shire/parish has a billboard for ads. Avoid using them elsewhere.

Booklets:

Pamphlet: 4-8 pages. 4x7 sizes, 60lb silk paper and saddle stitching – information.

Brochure: 8-16 pages. 5x8 sizes, 70lb silk paper and saddle stitching – services.

Catalogue: 16-32 pages. 6x9 sizes, 85lb silk paper and saddle stitching – products.

Lounging

Gazettes:

Puzzles: 24-48 pages. 4x7 sizes, 55lb paper and tape binding – crossword puzzles.

Sketches: 24-48 pages. 5x8 sizes, 60lb paper and tape binding – connect-the-dots.

Coloring: 24-48 pages. Use 6x9 sizes, 70lb paper and tape binding – coloring books.

Magazines:

Digest: 24-48 pages. 5x8 sizes, 60lb gloss paper, perfect binding – for children.

Comic: 24-48 pages. 6x9 sizes, 70lb gloss paper, perfect binding – for teenagers.

Popular: 24-48 pages. 8x10 sizes, 85lb gloss paper, perfect binding – for adults.

Directories:

Phone Book: 200-500 pages. 5.5x8.5 size, 40lb paper, paperback, no color.

Phone books with rain guards can be sent to mailboxes upon request.

Scholarly Individuals

Personal

Notebooks:

Sketchbooks: Professional drawings primarily for art classes. Use sewn binding.

Diary: Personal notebooks. Researchers use digital recorders. Use spiral binding.

Ledger: A book made of logs; customer paperwork is on tablets. Use coil binding.

Notes:

Post-It: Small adhesive reminders are used by office staff and for personal notes.

Cards: Cards serve as business cards, index cards for libraries and personal post cards.

Pad: Notepads are used by businesses and individuals to jot down important notes.

Letters:

Informal: Small, personal letters are used for RSVPs, reservations and sending invites.

Formal: Professional letters are sent out by various businesses and governments.

Epistle: Academic letters display penmanship skills with articles attached to them.

Luggage:

Folder: Folders are for legal paperwork. Businesses have the business tablets.

Binder: For students' tabs and papers. Businesses have the business tablets.

Briefcase: Used by business executives, jewelers and for banking purposes.

Loose:

Flyer: Flyers are passed out by freelancers marketing products and services.

Leaflet: Folded leaflets are passed out by nonprofit organizations as "PSAs".

Article: Academic reports are sent in to college admissions for entrance.

Articles use Times New Roman bodies, Arial titles and my book rules.

Digital Lounges

E-books

On the Go:

Subjects include poetry of the day, almanacs and handbooks. Follow similar formats. Use 5.5x8.5" page sizes and flip devices into landscape mode. Give them a one-page introduction, table of contents, synopsis/prologue, summary/epilogue, conclusion and a about the author. Use page breaks, overviews on title pages and two to five sections per chapter. Split chapters' last pages between their reviews and glossaries.

Audiobooks:

Audiobooks are ideal for insomniacs, the visually impaired, the lame who struggle to move and the mentally handicapped. These types of books will save those customers money. Now, they don't have to buy jumbo-sized disability print books! They support disability print just like any other e-book would. You can zoom in-and-out rapidly, bookmark, highlight and de-highlight at any time. A print book could never do that! The waterproof displays on devices prevent readers from degrading any of the pages.

Lounging

Digital Libraries:

Behind the ADMIN's kiosk, there are several tables set up for homework and essays. Past those tables, you'll see the reference section's bookcases. Behind the bookcases, the lounge is visible. The lounge is the farthest section in the library and when laid out correctly, has a window wall behind the sofas. They'll feature WIFI support and color tablets with headphones chained to the sofa section. This really benefits the visually impaired. Not only can they have really cool audiobooks at home, they can have them here too! There are magazines, listed earlier, the children could also read!

Digital Cafés:

Digital cafés following the plan above have an edge over the nonnatives. They need to support disability and audiobook readers. Offer cheaper coffee since coffee is way too expensive in this country. Make sure it's better also. Remember, while reading print books: Hold 3x6s with one hand near your eye, 4x7s with two hands, 5x8s with both elbows on the table, 6x9s with one hand as a chin rest while leaning in and 8x10s while leaning back without a chin rest. This renders disability font sizes obsolete.

Review

<u>Lounges</u>

Phone Books:

Paper boys could once again take to the streets making runs for businesses. Phone books will fair decently in the lounges of organizations just like landlines do. Not every business has a computer nearby to look something up on the internet and they shouldn't grant clerks the ability to use their personal cellphones while on duty. Also, the customers may need to make emergency calls if they don't have their cellphones.

The Magazines:

Many nonnative businesses do things backwards, like stocking books in their lounges while offering magazine subscriptions to homeowners. Magazines are much faster, cheaper and easier to produce. They allow readers access to quality paper and pictures, and new topics every week. Books can't compete with that! On the other hand, smaller, more affordable books can replace magazine subscriptions for homeowners. Yet, there'll always be that one business that wants books geared for their clients and homeowners who desire rotating topics for less money than books.

<u>Marketing</u>

Business Plans:

Big businesses often run television ads, smaller businesses sometimes buy radio ads and startup businesses might use billboards. Flyers are for freelance entrepreneurs. Be sure to print business cards, make a website and register your phone book listing.

Booklet Uses:

Smaller businesses will use booklets at their front desks as master copies and only hand out free flyers. More established corporations have discounts in bulk and give them away readily. If the business is information (white-collar), use pamphlets. If it's services (pink-collar), use brochures. If it's products (blue-collar), use catalogues.

CHAPTER TWELVE

Museum Consolidations

Overview

Defense

Lend-Lease:

Chapter Twelve discusses the strategic defense role of the United States' museums. Our military museums have almost a million tons of steel downrange and it takes a lot of time to produce ships during a world war. We don't have enough steel to make steel cars for everyone in the U.S. During the last world war, we placed rations on our steel and fuel. We seriously need to leverage some of the steel by remodeling excess ships back into our navy or by auctioning arms deals to developing allied countries.

The U.S. Navy:

The first book, Saving the United States, not only covered the country's public sector, it addressed their military too. My defense plan included flat-out buying most of the military museum exhibits so there would be less steel tied up in them. My goal is to only have the Midway fleet carrier, Texas super-dreadnought, North Carolina fast battleship, Salem heavy cruiser, Little Rock light cruiser and a handful of each type of ship as our naval museum exhibits. Scrap the Wasp LHDs; their steel is being wasted.

Setup

Relocation:

Relocating the museums to the strategic locations in this chapter allows them to become better secured against humidity, storm damage and enemy attacks. The locations aren't just a benefit to their protection, they're a benefit to their ability to be deployed quicker as well. When the time comes for a major war, we'll rent them.

Dinosaurs:

There are only so many full skeletons of certain dinosaur species. We can sell excess ones off to other countries who wish to build science museums. Now, every country can have various types of cool dinosaurs! The same concept applies to our art also.

Defense Plan

Rentals

Lend-Lease:

Our museum exhibits are leased, ideally during autumn and winter, for war and training purposes. Museum organizations will hold them during peak time periods and shall be compensated during the time they aren't available. The only time the military should lease the museums is during spring or summer, or during major wars.

Remodeling:

The Army Legion of Engineers will handle the technical work and guide the unskilled hands of the vagrant. Homeless people will be shipped in, and compensated with food and shelter while being stationed on the ships. During peak seasons, like spring and summer, shift remodeling towards the areas that the tourists don't see. During quieter seasons, like autumn and winter, remodel them more aggressively. Use the excess steel freed up to create arms deals for allies so you can pay for these projects.

Branch Duties:

The air force can handle the excess aviation exhibits, navy can handle excess warship exhibits and coast guard could handle the excess cutter exhibits. There aren't enough tank or artillery exhibits for the army to buy back or rent, so just leave them alone!

Upgrades

JSS Battleships:

The four Iowa-class and two South Dakota-class fast battleships will have their rear turrets replaced with entry ramps to garages. They'll run half of the length of each ship. Superstructures are remodeled with my lighter magnesium alloy. Crow's nests will have a radar replacing the black towers. All armor away from the turrets needs to be replaced with lighter composite armor. Turrets and magazines need their old armor's weight to manage recoil. Replace the turrets' 5" guns with magnum 4" guns.

LHD Carriers:

The four Essex-class carriers will be hollowed-out so they can have a garage. They'll have well docks with front-and-rear doors and ski jump-style ramps for STOBAR. (short take-off but arrested recovery) Their flight decks have composite armor.

Military Museums

Aircraft Museum

Fargo, North Dakota:

Fargo will have the national air museum. Their stealth exhibit section will contain every type of cool reconnaissance and stealth aircraft. B1 Lancers will be present too.

Sioux Falls, South Dakota:

This U.S. Air Force base will serve as the national boneyard. It'll be kept empty and process decommissioned airplanes into allied arms deals or parts for civilian aircraft.

Tank Museum

Richmond, Virginia:

Relocate the Patton Tank Museum here. Move the ground vehicles into a climate-controlled warehouse to better preserve them and cut down on future maintenance.

Langley, Virginia:

This army base will serve as the national military junkyard. It'll be kept empty and process decommissioned vehicles into allied arms deals or scrapyard parts for cars.

Naval Museum

Pearl Harbor, Hawaii:

The Nimitz Naval Museum goes here. It houses all of the military museum ships and boats. It's an area that has low humidity and great weather. During war, the navy rents their ships and returns them when they're not needed. If an exhibit is lost at sea, the museum is reimbursed full-market-value with inflation adjustment for it. Carriers serve on the line of battle, subs deploy SEALs and noncapital ships escort convoys. Battleships handle shore bombardment, fast combat support and rescues.

Suisan Bay, California:

This naval base currently serves as our national mothball fleet. It'll be kept empty and process all decommissioned watercraft into allied arms deals or parts for boaters.

National Museums

Showcases

The Art Museum:

Consolidate all of our preexisting art museums into Manhattan, New York City.

The Science Museum:

Consolidate all preexisting science museums into central Trenton, New Jersey.

The Train Museum:

Consolidate all preexisting train museums into Philadelphia, Pennsylvania.

The Car Museum:

Consolidate all preexisting car museums into downtown Detroit, Michigan.

The Toy Museum:

Relocate all museum grade toys into downtown Providence, Rhode Island.

Identity

The Dakotas:

Each of our states need to have their own identity, tourist attractions and economic sustainability. Right now, the Dakotas are the weakest, especially North Dakota. The new U.S. Air Force museum will increase tourism, revenue and population statewide.

Their Locations:

The reason why I picked Rhode Island for the toys is because the region surrounding it was the most famous area for children's toys in the country. Detroit was chosen over Indiana and Florida because they made the cars for those race tracks in the first place. Pennsylvania's railroads have the most fame and history and are a good choice. New York, New York is famous for their artists, fashion designers and runway shows.

Our Military:

Virginia is near the capitol where remembering veterans and infantry is the strongest. Pearl Harbor is the biggest naval region in the country and already has our naval memorial. Suisan Bay, California is already our main mothball base and serves as the area for the reserve fleet. You couldn't relocate these facilities even if you tried!

Review

Preservation

Nuclear Retirement:

If the nuclear-powered ships from my first book's military inventory lists retire again, the nuclear fuel could be stripped out of them by NEST teams without incurring additional costs during decommissioning. Make sure your thorium reactors obey the designs from Chapter Seven: Resource Management. Civilian ships use the same steam turbines, boilers and hydrogen pilot lights used on the navy's nuclear-powered ships. Their boats use hydrogen for their hybrid-electric V10s with cylinder shutoff.

Consolidations:

A smaller handful of larger museums are better than a larger quantity of smaller ones. They'll have higher quality exhibits since there are only so many T-Rex skeletons or battleships to look at. If you had a bunch of smaller ones, they'll need to fill up their museums with exhibits and by doing so, lower their standards to meet their quotas. Many of the things you see today in most modern art museums shouldn't even be considered art, let alone history! They can afford to hire more staff to maintain them due to the greater revenue they'll generate. They won't require subsidies anymore.

Sales

Exportation:

There are two metals freed up with this plan: steel and aluminum. The steel will be used to manufacture arms deals for allied countries. Excess aluminum is used in a similar fashion for building military aircraft for allied countries. There's so much aluminum that you'll have to make other things for the civilians as well. You could generate revenue by bolstering up the aviation and car companies. Encourage car companies to use steel frames and aluminum bodies. This lowers future vehicle costs and prevents them from becoming too light. Also, the smallest countries will have dinosaurs for their kids now! Every little boy should be able to see at least one.

Summary

Wolf Execution

Recap

This concludes my presentation of *Native American Strategies*, the ultimate handbook on all things private sector and improving personal lives for Native Americans! Without this book, it would have been much harder to execute Operation White Wolf and propel your Native American leaders into office. Now, they can enact the plans from the first book with impunity. The private sector shall become yours!

Rehash

There'll come time periods where you'll wish to read portions of this book again. There were three steps spread out across three generations time. It's only natural to rehash on these topics, especially when answering questions or imparting wisdom to your children. Just like how Native American politicians will hide a copy of the first book in their office, stash this book in yours. Guard these secrets with your life! If you haven't picked up a copy of Saving the United States, please do so. It teaches you how to balance the political lean in the government so you can pass or block its laws.

Closing

The last step is the *Inside Out Method*. It's a dating book that can help boost your population. There's an e-book version built for cellphones for "on-the-go" use. As the principal investigator and sole researcher of this project, I'm signing off now. If you still need more resources, feel free to read my online bibliographies at any time.

Conclusion

Afterword

Thank you for reading his book! When Robert started this project, he didn't have a grant or a research team to help him. This man couldn't work for several years due to physical ailments. He didn't receive any unemployment, welfare or disability from the government while conducting his research. The author had to live off of less than $100 a week while writing his books. Your support not only furthers the author's research, but also helps the indigenous people of the New World break free from the Anglo-Saxons ruling over them.

-N.D.

Postface

TAX TREES originally started out as TREES FOR TAXES, a tax-deductible native landscaping program. I wanted to encourage the people from Montgomery County, TX to replant native forestry plants on their property in an attempt to combat the urbanization destroying my lands. That failed and later became the Landscaper's Bible, a forestry research book. Then, it evolved into a plan on how to pay off the national debt. Once that failed, I knew I had to do something. So, I decided to help the natives kick these idiots off their land!

-R.R.

Acknowledgements

I would like to thank GOTCHA! LLP for their editorial services and Kindle Direct Publishing for publishing all of my books. Special thanks go out to Streetlight Graphics for designing the signature "money tree" illustration for me. Special mention to Unsplash.com for their premium digital photography used on all of my books. Each of their photographers will be given credit on my website.

I personally thank each and every reader for reading my second book! Most importantly, I would like to thank God. If it weren't for his guidance, I would have never been capable of creating these models on my own. God bless!

<u>Native American Strategies</u>

"The handbook that teaches Native Americans how to take over the private sector's businesses and pump resources back into their communities!"

CONTRIBUTIONS

Subsection Index

About the Author

My name is Robert Robinson. My background started out as a cowboy when I was in elementary school working on my family's ranch. When I hit middle school, I joined the Civil Air Patrol. The air force auxiliary motivated me to study the military because it interested me. In high school, I ran my own landscaping business called Robinson's Landscaping. It was never legally incorporated and rarely had more than two full-time employees working.

I graduated from the class of 2005 at Montgomery High School in Montgomery, TX. For college, I attended The Art Institute of Houston twice for applied science. First, I received my associate degree in Restaurant Catering and Management. Second, I received my bachelors in Hospitality Management. I worked as a line cook and expeditor during the time I spent in the culinary industry. After that, I started focusing on my research books.

I've played drums since 2000 and am an avid music enthusiast. I also diet and weight train as my personal form of physical rehabilitation. I'm using my experience and research in lieu of education to hit post-doctoral topics.

Glossary

Bass String Instruments

Soundboards generate sound vibrations. They're found on the stringed instruments in orchestras. For example: pianos, harpsicords and violins. Bass plates are strength rods. *Remember that: blocks = frames, linings = bindings and bass plates = dowels.*

Cage-Free

Cage-free free-range eggs require hens that aren't locked in cages giving them plenty of exercise and play. A happier hen will make orange egg yolks, not the yellow ones!

Dust Jacket

This is the removable cover on a hardback book. If they're glued on, the book will be ruined if the dust jacket gets torn off. They were designed to be replaceable. Fiction books using raised text will place the raised text on either the cover or the dust jacket.

Free-Ranging

Urban free-ranging is used for rabbits, quail and flightless pheasant since they're too vulnerable to be continuously left in the pasture due to predators. They're given organic pellets, cereals, fruit and veggies. Hobby farms' horses are also free-ranged.

100% Grass-Fed

The 100% grass-fed rating involves ranchers grazing hooved animals out to pasture to munch on whatever they find, and giving them hay and crops. Both food sources are naturally made from fields. They're labeled "100% grass-fed and grass-finished".

Hard/Paper Back

This is often called a hardcover or a softcover. Anything "back" is the manuscript era (modern) and anything "cover" is codex era (metal or leather cover, often blank) style cover. Say paperback (not softcover) and hardback (not hardcover) for these books.

Hard/Soft Cover

This is the codex-style cover. It's either blank, made of leather (softcover), metal or hand-carved from hardwoods. The plural form of the word codex is spelt "codices".

Musical Bridges

Bridges carry sound to soundboards. They look like the Golden Gate bridge, are on orchestral bass string instruments, inside pianos and at the bases of guitar strings.

Natural Rating

Used on the park system's timber plots. Timber is sprayed with natural plant-based treatment and sealant once harvested. Choosing natural ratings on timber are better for the environment they grow in. This reduces chemicals found in their rain runoff.

Non-GMO Rating

For plant or fungi-based pesticides, antibiotics, medicines, fertilizers and rooting hormones. Selective breeding shall replace all GMOs. GMO stands for genetically modified organism. Avoid the usage of synthetics or chemicals to qualify for this rating. This rating is usually displayed on farm supplies, not the consumers' products.

Organic Rating

Used on all farms. Medicinal herbs are used to make antibiotics. Plants are used to make pesticides. Duck runs help eliminate some of the pests before organic plant-based pesticides are used. Compost, aged manure and worm castings are used for fertilizer. Rooting stocks from willows and cloned plant cuttings will replace all GMOs.

Pastured Poultry

The pastured poultry rating involves ranchers sending their birds out to eat nothing else besides what they can find in the pasture. They go in after the grass-fed animals lower the grass height to a medium-height. Pastured poultry cannot have any pellets, but pastured hooved animals can. This has to do with the rating system's structure.

Piano Construction

Pin locks are inside pianos and are the tuning pins holding the strings. The plate is the huge, often orange and colorful metal thingy underneath the lid holding the strings. It looks like a harp and the bridge is located below this. The lyres are the piano pedals.

Premium Color

Premium color is used on photography since they're more modern, have sharper lines and more saturated colors on images. Premium color requires heavier paper choices in order to prevent the ink from bleeding through the other side of the pages.

Scritta Paper

Scritta paper is often called bible paper. Scritta is the proper term, not that long sentence-sized term they changed it to now. It's made out of cotton instead of wood.

Standard Color

Standard color is used on illustrations since they're either old-fashioned or feature rounded edges. Premium color often looks too modern and bleeds through on lighter paper. Lighter paper choices allow bigger books, like textbooks for example, to become thinner, lighter and cheaper to produce, to distribute and carry around.

Colophon

Graphic Design Group

Graphic Design, Covers

TAX TREES: THE LANDSCAPER'S BIBLE, (ed. 3)

TAX TREES: SAVING THE UNITED STATES, (ed. 1)

TAX TREES: NATIVE AMERCIAN STRATEGIES, (ed. 1)

Kindle Direct Publishing

Publishing, Marketing

TAX TREES: technical handbook trilogy (ed. 1-2)

BJÖRK'S ADVENTURE, parody thriller novel (ed. 1)

MY DIRE STRAITS, author's memoir (ed. 1-2)

CANNABIS MARKET, technical handbook (ed. 1)

THE EARLY CHURCH, technical handbook (ed. 1)

Amazon.com, Inc.

Printing, Distribution

TAX TREES: THE LANDSCAPER'S BIBLE, (ed. 1-3)

TAX TREES, technical handbook trilogy (ed. 1)

BJÖRK'S ADVENTURE, parody thriller novel (ed. 1)

MY DIRE STRAITS, author's memoir (ed. 1)

CANNABIS MARKET, technical handbook (ed. 1)

THE EARLY CHURCH, technical handbook (ed. 1)

2012 Copyright: TXU 1-821-070

https://robertrobinsonjr.com

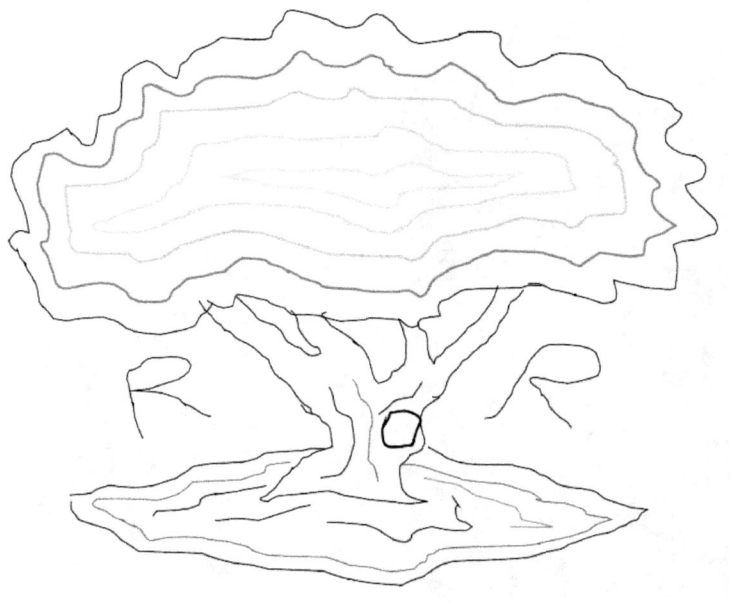